American United Life Insurance Company®

Progress Through Partnership

1877 – 2002

American United Life Insurance Company®

Progress Through Partnership

1877 – 2002

James R. Hetherington

Guild Press Emmis Publishing LP

GUILD PRESS EMMIS PUBLISHING LP
10665 Andrade Drive
Zionsville, Indiana 46077
317-733-4175

ISBN 1-57860-116-9
Library of Congress Catalog Card Number 2002107997

Interior and text design by Sheila G. Samson
Dust jacket design by Listenberger Design Associates

Printed in China

CONTENTS

Foreword

Any story about American United Life Insurance Company must begin with people and values. From its beginnings in 1877 as a fraternal organization—where life insurance was introduced for the protection of its members—to the diverse financial services organization of 2002, trusted partnerships have been the foundation of AUL and its predecessors. While the pages of this book contain generations of history about AUL and the people who have contributed to the company's highly successful century-and-a-quarter of keeping promises to its customers, the real story is what the company and its people are doing today to ensure good stewardship and value in the future. The world has changed, the business environment has changed and the industry has changed, and all three will continue to do so at a pace that will boggle our minds.

People, values, and a willingness to anticipate and respond to this change will determine which companies survive—and thrive—in the coming years. On December 17, 2000, AUL completed the most significant undertaking in the company's history, restructuring as a mutual insurance holding company (MHC). This hybrid organization gives our customers and our company the best of both worlds—retained ownership at the top of the organization with the flexibility to issue stock through our subsidiaries should the need for additional capital arise. We are no longer just an insurance company. We are a financial services enterprise with partner companies whose strengths will compliment AUL's strengths for the benefit of all our stakeholders.

As a result of our restructuring, a new company—OneAmerica Financial Partners, Inc.—was created. OneAmerica™ will be the enterprise brand and identity under which all of our MHC partners will rally. AUL and our partner companies will still be around and will continue to take care of our customers and the relationships that have been built over many years. But OneAmerica will provide us with a sense of unity and a more effective and efficient way to operate our businesses.

OneAmerica aspires to be dynamic, innovative and responsive—the qualities we believe today's business- and technology-savvy customers not only expect, but demand. But the values that have guided AUL and its predecessor companies for 125 years have not really changed. For a half-century AUL has been known as the "Company with the Partnership Philosophy," and that philosophy continues to guide us today.

With this book, *American United Life Insurance Company: Progress Through Partnership, 1877–2002*, we honor our past for it is the foundation upon which we seek to build our future: One focus. One vision. OneAmerica.

James W. Freeman
Vice President, Corporate Communications

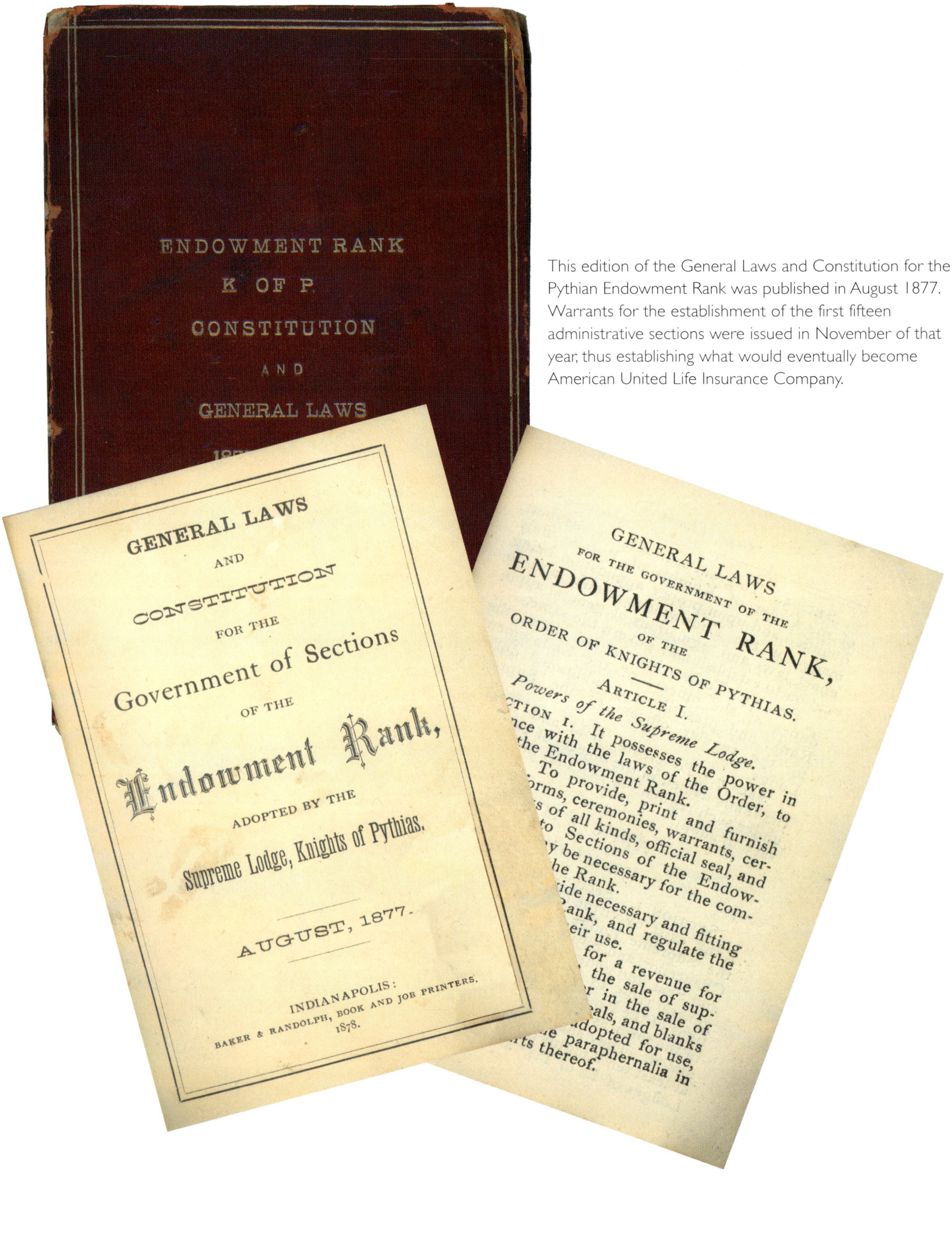

This edition of the General Laws and Constitution for the Pythian Endowment Rank was published in August 1877. Warrants for the establishment of the first fifteen administrative sections were issued in November of that year, thus establishing what would eventually become American United Life Insurance Company.

CHAPTER I

THE DAYS OF KNIGHTS

In 1877—twelve years after the Civil War ended—the nation was still very much divided and life uncertain. Rutherford B. Hayes took office following a bitterly contested election that was so close it was decided on a partisan vote by a congressional committee. Both North and South had recently experienced devastating financial crises. Millions of blacks remained unintegrated into society in a South that had not recovered from Reconstruction. Illness and early death were fearsome specters, with yellow fever epidemics common and tuberculosis a leading cause of death. Every fifth child still died in infancy.

In the move toward westward expansion, Indian wars were claiming many lives, including the year before at the Battle of the Little Big Horn those of General George Custer and his 264 Seventh Cavalrymen.

It was in this atmosphere that the Supreme Lodge of the Knights of Pythias convened on an August morning in the new Cuyahoga County Courthouse in Cleveland, Ohio, to create a life insurance plan for members of the fraternal order as a societal response to the uncertainties of the day.

At the Knights of Pythias convention the year before in Philadelphia, a proposal to make insurance assessments compulsory on the general membership had been strongly rejected. As the minutes reported, the committee on law had "literally torn to shreds" a proposed constitution of the Minnesota Knights of Pythias Widows and Orphans Relief Fund.

One speaker called the insurance plan "a most dangerous cargo to place aboard our Pythian craft." The record mentioned "the worship of Mammon" and suggested that such a scheme would act like a "fungous growth" that absorbs all the "life blood of the tree and causes its destruction." They feared the financial risks and responsibilities an insurance program would place on a relatively small organization.

The intervening year, however, had seen several forces work to change members' attitudes. The severe depression that had begun in 1873 continued to retard business prosperity, and membership was suffering because many Pythians simply could not afford to belong. Benefits like insurance would appeal to would-be members. There was great appeal in the insurance programs being offered by other fraternal orders.

In the era following the Civil War, when most Americans worked either on farms or as laborers in industry, they recognized the need for insurance protection. They could not, however, afford, at their low wages, to protect their families with the insurance offered by private companies. Moreover, many Americans, who distrusted insurance firms, could not understand the necessity for the reserve accumulations required by a private insurer, and the failure of several insurance firms in the financial panics following the Civil War deepened their distrust.

Family men were much more likely to put their faith in an insurance program operated by a fraternal order, where a man's protection was controlled by loyal lodge brothers, and low-cost mutual insurance plans were a strong inducement to membership.

So, on that August morning in 1877, the Supreme Chancellor of the Knights of Pythias, Stillman S. Davis, told the gathering, "There is now a strong desire that some (insurance) plan may be adopted . . . which shall be universal in its application and management, with all those who shall voluntarily enter into it. I believe this can be done in no way so well . . . as to create a Rank that shall cover this whole question and embrace all the wise features of other organizations. I would recommend that this subject be referred to a special committee early in the session, and that they be requested to report at the earliest moment possible."

Chancellor Davis, a Civil War Navy veteran from New Hampshire, saw the need for an insurance program as "vital," saying, "it will prevent our members seeking other organizations that have this feature so prominent" and ". . . it would create an interest in the Order, which nothing else could." He cited letters in which Pythian officers and prominent members warned that, if

In his report to the Supreme Lodge meeting in 1877, Supreme Chancellor Stillman S. Davis made an urgent appeal to the body to adopt some system of life insurance. He claimed it was vital to the interests of the order, saying, "I have received some letters from officers and prominent members of different jurisdictions, saying if some steps are not taken soon by the Supreme Lodge in this direction, their lodges, both Grand and Subordinate, will cease to exist." His appeal produced the desired effect. Davis, from Nashua, New Hampshire, served as Supreme Chancellor from 1874 to 1878.

some steps were not taken soon in the direction of an insurance system, their lodges would cease to exist.

Responding to this dramatic warning, Representative James W. Mavity of Louisville, Kentucky, stood up the next day, August 15, and presented a resolution that a committee of three be appointed to prepare an insurance proposal. In an evening session two days later, the report of the Special Committee on Endowment, headed by the founder of the Knights of Pythias, Justus H. Rathbone, was adopted by a vote of 56 to 6. It recommended "the adoption of an endowment scheme, a participation in the benefits of which shall be optional with each member of the Knight's rank (full membership) and shall be secured by membership in the Endowment Rank. . . ."

Following the committee's recommendations, a five-man committee was appointed to perfect the Endowment Rank. Rathbone chaired the committee, which also included Samuel P. Oyler of Indiana, W. Bryce Thompson of Tennessee, George W. Griffiths of Kentucky, and Leander Firestone of Ohio. The Supreme Chancellor, Vice Chancellor, Master of Exchequer, and Keeper of Records and Seal were ex-officio members. The Master of Exchequer was John B. Stumph of Indianapolis, Indiana.

Meeting the day after the convention adjourned and at length in late September, the committee formulated a ritual, an installation service for officers, general laws and a constitution for the Rank. They were formally promulgated in a circular issued October 1, 1877, over the seal of the Supreme Chancellor. Complete with a lengthy initiation service that included raps, passwords, a grip, and signs of recognition, courtesy, caution and distress, the new Rank designated that its members be hailed as "Companion."

A belief grew over the years that the Pythian Endowment Rank was

After the Supreme Keeper of Records and Seal declined to handle the clerical duties of the new Endowment Rank, John B. Stumph, the Supreme Master of Exchequer, was asked to accept the job and he did. "Fortunately so," wrote Pythian historian William D. Kennedy, because in his opinion Stumph "was a man of fine business ability, sterling integrity, sound judgment, and one who would not be swerved from the path of rectitude." Stumph, who was born in Germany, came to America in 1838 and to Indianapolis in 1843. He was one of the early members of Marion Lodge No. 1 in Indianapolis, and served as the Knights of Pythias' Supreme Master of Exchequer from 1874 to 1884. He died in 1903.

chartered by an act of Congress passed on November 7, 1877. When the subject was investigated in 1967, no such charter could be found. But the active life of the Pythian Endowment Rank did in fact begin in November 1877. Warrants for the establishment of the first fifteen administrative sections were issued on November 15 that year, and the first two sections were actually instituted on November 27. It could be that the latter date was miscopied as November 7, giving rise to the long-held founding date. (Congress did incorporate the Supreme Lodge Knights of Pythias in an act passed and signed by President Grover Cleveland in 1894.)

In any event, the history of what would eventually become American United Life Insurance Company began in November 1877 as the Endowment Rank of the Knights of Pythias. At the time, the fraternal order, which had been founded in 1864, had more than 92,000 members and had become an international organization.

The system for insurance protection created by the new Rank's constitution was relatively simple. The Rank was composed of sections, each with no fewer than seven members. Only Pythians who were members in good standing of the Order's Chivalric Rank and who were not over fifty years of age were to be admitted, and admittance also depended on the approval of a committee of investigation, the recommendation of an examining physician, a vote of the membership, and payment of the necessary fee.

Some artifacts from the early days of the Knights of Pythias insurance program.

The logo of the Endowment Rank emphasized the lodge's credo of friendship, charity, and benevolence.

When the Knights of Pythias began offering life insurance to its members, hand posting in ledgers such as this was the standard method of record keeping and accounting, a slow and tedious process.

Unfortunately, the constitution provided that, until June 1, 1878, "all members of the Knights of Pythias may become members of the Endowment Rank without regard to age, provided they possess the other required qualifications." The intent was to allow older men who were members on October 1, 1877, the opportunity to participate in the insurance program, but the result was a rush of nonmembers into existing lodges and even the establishment of new lodges of older brand-new members, all seeking to be eligible for the Endowment Rank. It would allow them to get reasonably priced insurance.

An admission fee of three dollars was the only initial cost of membership in the Endowment Rank and bought one thousand dollars of protection under its life insurance plan. Of this fee, one dollar was retained in the section treasury for expenses. The other two were forwarded to the Supreme Master of Exchequer (treasurer of the order), the capable John B. Stumph of Indianapolis. Of the two dollars, one was deposited in the Endowment Fund, out of which death benefits were paid, and the other went into the Rank's Expense Fund.

Membership in the Endowment Rank was divided into First and Second Classes, paying death benefits of $1,000 and $2,000, respectively. A member could belong to either or both classes but could not hold two memberships in the same class. Whenever there were fewer than one thousand members in the First Class or two thousand in the Second, the constitution stated that a death benefit in either should be paid on the basis of one dollar for each member. However, after one year of operation, the Endowment Rank had more than three thousand certificate holders in the First Class and more than five thousand in the Second.

Fortunately, with nine death claims in the Second Class that first year, the constitution empowered the Supreme Master of Exchequer to assess each member of a class $1.25 whenever the class fund, because of payment of a death claim, fell below the amount needed to pay the next. But, even with that assistance, Stumph had to borrow $925 from the Second Class Expense Fund to pay the ninth death benefit of that first year.

The addition of the Endowment Rank and its insurance program spurred the growth of membership in the Knights of Pythias. The order once more became one of the nation's most prominent fraternal organizations. Pythians in one two-year period added 110,117 men to their ranks, and on the eve of the order's thirtieth birthday in 1893 it had 393,716 dues-paying members.

The rapid and widespread growth of the Endowment Rank revealed shortcomings in its structure that stemmed from the lack of expertise among its creators. A Pythian historian, William D. Kennedy, later wrote that the Rank was "directed and handled by men who, while they may have been capable in their respective business callings, were absolutely inexperienced and untaught in the science of insurance."

Kennedy did pay tribute to the Rank's first financial manager, Supreme

The Indiana Pythian Building was an Indianapolis landmark, frequently referred to as the "flatiron building" because of its triangular shape resulting from its location at the intersection of Pennsylvania Street and Massachusetts Avenue. When it was completed in 1907, the $450,000 structure was described as the costliest and most handsome Knights of Pythias building in the world.

Noted Hoosier artist Harry A. Davis was commissioned by American United Life Insurance Company to do this painting of the flatiron building. Davis graduated from Herron School of Art (now part of IUPUI) and taught for thirty-seven years. He has received many national and international awards for his artwork. The painting is part of AUL's extensive art collection.

Master of Exchequer John Stumph, saluting his practicality, common sense and integrity as well as his stubbornness. Stumph, a German-born merchant who settled in Indianapolis in 1843, bluntly pointed out to the Supreme Chancellor in his first financial report the obvious shortcomings of the insurance program. These included a looseness in admitting members, which he illustrated by citing two 1878 deaths from delirium tremens, surely a diagnosable condition.

Other problems he mentioned included lack of central control of admissions and the loose wording of the Rank's constitution that permitted the influx of members over the age of fifty during the first months of the Rank's existence. Stumph battled to improve the administration of the Rank until 1884, when he stepped down as Supreme Master of Exchequer.

By 1880 the need for improvements in the administration of the Endowment Rank was critical, and a number of recommendations from an Endowment Rank committee were adopted that year at the Supreme Lodge convention in St. Louis. A Board of Control was established, consisting of two members of the Supreme Lodge plus the Supreme Chancellor as chairman. It was to supervise the general management of the Rank.

The appointment was authorized of a medical examiner-in-chief, whose decision on the physical eligibility of an applicant would be final. The first doctor to hold the post was Dr. J. W. Taylor of Indianapolis. A code of laws governing medical examinations was also adopted, and application blanks were made more detailed.

A new Third Class of membership in the Rank was established at the 1880 convention for members between fifty and sixty years of age. Its death benefit was one thousand dollars or "so much thereof as there were members in this class."

Four years later the Supreme Lodge, meeting in New Orleans, abolished the ritual connected with the Endowment Rank and authorized the election of the first Supreme Secretary, Halvor Nelson. It also created a new Fourth Class of membership, based on graded assessments.

This marked change in the approach to insurance reflected recognition of defects inherent in a system based on a uniform assessment. As the average age of Rank members had increased, special assessments became more frequent, and younger members realized they were paying an amount out of proportion to the degree of their risk. They began to drop out of the Rank, and the Pythians, like other fraternal orders, were forced to develop a system of graded assessments.

Members of the Fourth Class could elect a death benefit of $1,000, $2,000 or $3,000, at an entrance fee of two dollars for each thousand dollars of coverage. Thereafter, they made monthly payments for life at a set level based on their age at entry. Based on American tables of mortality and the Endowment Rank's six years of experience, payments per $1,000 of benefit ranged from 70 cents monthly at admission age of 21 to $8.30 at age 79. These monthly payments were divided between an endowment fund and a reserve, the latter being invested by the Supreme Master of Exchequer after operating expenses were paid. From this reserve would be paid death benefits when current deaths made the endowment funds insufficient.

The new Fourth Class was a much more scientific approach to the writing of life insurance, but there were still problems. Members of the first three classes were admitted into the new class without reexaminations and on the basis of the age they had been when admitted to the older class. This led to serious actuarial problems, and the Supreme Lodge realized it had acted without the adequate actuarial expertise that made private insurance companies successful.

By 1888 the situation had reached crisis proportions because of insufficient rates. The Supreme Chancellor called for a "radical change . . . in the system adopted," and the Endowment Rank committee responded with a new code of laws and other changes in governing the Rank. The Board of Control was made elective and was to have sole direction of the Rank. It was to re-rate the transferred Fourth Class members so that they would thereafter pay assessments at rates based on their age when they entered the new class.

Then a new problem emerged as the popularity of the Endowment Rank insurance plan increased. The fraternal order's initials, emblems, and mottoes were freely borrowed by commercial firms, particularly those dealing in life and accident insurance.

A particular offender was the Pythian Life Association of Omaha, Nebraska, which refused to recognize the authority of the Supreme Lodge or to change its name. In 1892 the Knights angrily passed strong resolutions prohibiting such unauthorized use of the order's name, derivatives and insignia and, by threatening legal action, forced the offenders to cease and desist.

Despite financial crises caused in 1893 by unwise investments and in 1901 by an apparent embezzlement, the Knights of Pythias and its Endowment Rank continued to grow, the latter gaining sophistication as an insuring organization. In 1901 however, for the first time in its history, the Supreme Lodge was called to a special convention—to deal with problems of the Endowment Rank. At that meeting in Chicago, the Board of Control reported it had death losses of $425,000 and no funds to pay them. John A. Hinsey of Illinois, who had headed the Endowment Rank Board of Control, resigned, and Charles F. S. Neal, an insurance agent from Lebanon, Indiana, was named to succeed him.

The special convention voted to "produce full and prompt payment of all claims," and it adopted the rate schedule recommended by the National Fraternal Congress on the basis of the table of mortality it had developed in the late 1890s. The Congress, an association of 12 fraternal benefit societies, realized that the financial solvency of the fraternal programs depended on the use of scientific methods in setting rates and in providing reserves. Statistics of 25 commercial companies and 27 fraternal benefit societies were tabulated and compared, and the table of mortality was created. This was a major step in setting the fraternal organizations on a sound actuarial basis.

The Level Life Table, based on age, occupation and medical selection, meant an increase of 45 percent in the monthly assessments paid by Endowment Rank members, but it was adopted with the proviso that, if and when the condition of the Rank's finances warranted it, the order could suspend collection of monthly assessments.

The next year at the Supreme Lodge convention, Hoosier Charles F. S. Neal was re-elected president of the Board of Control, and it was reported that 58,169 of 540,138 Pythians belonged to the Endowment Rank. At the turn of the century, more than 300 fraternal societies counted an estimated four million members, who carried some $6 billion in insurance. Five years later, the number of societies had practically doubled; membership had grown to more than six million and insurance in force to $8 billion.

The Knights of Pythias and its insurance program grew along with the other fraternal orders in the United States, but, in those first years of the twentieth century, fraternal insurance received its share of criticism and attack, just as did private companies.

The Michigan insurance commissioner was an especially outspoken critic, charging that fraternal insurance was only temporary indemnity, not insurance for life. He claimed that officers had improperly used reserve funds, had borrowed from mortuary and reserve funds, and paid themselves large and handsome salaries. Newspapers joined the attack. One editor, responding to a lodge officer's contention that a state had no right to regulate the nonprofit fraternal insurance programs, wrote that they were "just as rightly the subject of attack as the Louisiana Lottery or any other fraud invented by avarice or ignorance for the purpose of bringing about a speedier separation of a fool and his money."

As one of the large fraternal orders, the Knights of Pythias received its share of criticism, but to its credit the order again took wisely planned action to analyze and restructure the Endowment Rank. In 1904 Supreme Chancellor Tracy R. Bangs appointed a special committee to make a detailed study of the insurance program.

The committee hired the New York actuarial firm of Wolfe and Wolfe to assist in the analysis. Its recommendations, approved at the order's next biennial convention, held in 1906 in New Orleans, transformed the Endowment Rank into a full-fledged and soundly structured legal reserve fraternal insurance organization. The Endowment Rank was now the Insurance Department of the Knights of Pythias.

Since 1884 the active membership in the insurance program had been in the Rank's Fourth Class, which had absorbed members of the earlier three classes. The committee recommended continuation of the Fourth Class but proposed that a new Fifth Class be organized to begin operation January 1, 1907.

It offered to members between the ages of 21 and 60 certificates ranging from $500 to $5,000 in four plans of insurance: level life plan, 20-year payment plan, modified step-rate plan, and level plan to age 65. The rates for each plan were based on the American Experience Table of Mortality. Current members of the Fourth Class could transfer at their attained age to the Fifth Class without expense or medical examination if they did so before January 1, 1909, or thereafter upon passage of a medical examination. Fifth Class members could hold certificates in more than one plan so long as the total insurance did not exceed $5,000.

All of the plans except the modified step-rate plan provided for the accumulation of a reserve that was to be augmented at 3 percent a year. After three years, this reserve could be used to purchase extended or paid-up insurance when members were unable to continue their payments, thus preventing forfeiture and loss of reserve share.

At the end of each year, a valuation and accounting would be made on all certificates. If the actual mortality cost, actual operating expense and necessary reserve were less than the amount collected, the excess would be applied to the next year's payments. Thus members were assured of safe and permanent protection at absolute cost, and no "eminently unfair" surpluses accumulated.

Eventually the Fourth Class was re-rated and also based on the American Experience Table of Mortality. Safeguards were incorporated to protect the investment of funds, and Pythians at last had a stable, soundly based insurance program as secure as any offered by private companies.

As the "Endowment Rank" was transformed into the "Insurance Department," the Indiana Grand Lodge of the Knights of Pythias was constructing an eleven-story home for itself in Indianapolis. Financed and built by Harry Wade, Grand Keeper of Records and Seals, the triangular edifice at the intersection of Massachusetts Avenue and Pennsylvania Street was the tallest structure in the city at the time.

The new landmark was a distinguished building of blue and buff Indiana limestone, and when it was dedicated August 12–17, 1907, the *Insurance Department News* reported:

" . . . now one Grand Lodge builds a magnificent temple and office building in a great, modern American city, excelling, overtopping and exceeding all other buildings in the city! Pythianism is a great living principle and, lo! its stream runs here and there and everywhere, and its bosom is covered by sails of every craft and upon every banner thereon is the motto: 'Friendship, Charity and Benevolence.' "

The new building did indeed warrant some degree of that enthusiasm. It was of fireproof steel construction in a most advanced design and contained its own pair of driven water wells, its own power generating equipment, and a forced-air filtering system that cleaned, humidified, and circulated air through its eleven floors.

The street floor housed a series of shops with display windows both on the

The American Experience Table of Mortality, one of the best-known of all mortality tables, was published in 1868. It is based upon the experience of the Mutual Life Insurance Company of New York from 1843 to 1858 and includes all the accumulated experience of the company from the inception of operations. It was later supplanted by tables developed under the aegis of the National Association of Insurance Commissioners.

exterior and in an interior arcade decorated with mosaic flooring and marble wainscoting. It included a candy store, shoe store and lunchroom, while the basement contained a handsome cafe and a Turkish bath. Staircases and four elevators gave access to more than 300 offices on the first eight floors above, which were finished in golden oak. The Pythian emblem decorated all the hardware and electrical fixtures, as it did the elegant green-and-gold auditorium that occupied the tenth and eleventh floors. The auditorium was surrounded by smaller meeting rooms.

Harry Wade, who later became president of the Knights of Pythias Insurance Department, interested the lodge in moving its Insurance Department to Indianapolis and in becoming the tenant on the ninth floor of the new building. It moved there in April 1910. The Endowment Rank had been based in Indianapolis when John Stumph was Supreme Master of Exchequer, but it was headquartered in Washington, D.C., from 1884 to 1889 and in Chicago from 1889 until its return to the Hoosier capital in 1910.

From 1907 to 1914, the Knights of Pythias added 100,000 new members, and by 1921 it boasted a membership above 900,000. Insurance written annually by the Order rose from $5,293,000 in 1918 to $13,336,500 in 1921.

Harry Wade was a watchmaker and jeweler in Lafayette, Indiana, when in 1903 he was elected Grand Keeper of Records and Seals of the Indiana Grand Lodge of the Knights of Pythias, which prompted a move to Indianapolis. He later conceived the idea of an Indiana Pythian Building in the capital, personally raised the money to get it built, and then got the lodge to move its Insurance Department from Chicago to that building. He was elected president of the Insurance Department in 1915 and president of United Mutual Life Insurance Company in 1930, when the Insurance Department was separated from the lodge. He died in 1933.

Union B. Hunt, a former Indiana secretary of state and chairman of the Railroad Commission of Indiana, was president of the Knights of Pythias Insurance Department from 1908 to 1915. He played an important role in the organization's move to Indianapolis in 1910. The Insurance Department had been based in Chicago.

Damon, Pythias, and Justus

The ancient legend of two close friends, Damon and Pythias, was popularized in mid-nineteenth-century America by Irish playwright John Banim, and the story helped inspire Justus Henry Rathbone when he formed the Knights of Pythias fraternal order in 1864.

A year earlier, Rathbone, then a twenty-four-year-old clerk in the U.S. Surgeon General's office in Washington, D.C., conceived the idea of forming, as he said to some associates, an order based on some "brotherly love story." He was especially anxious that the name should have the prefix "Knights."

He kept harping on this idea, according to Pythian historian William D. Kennedy, ". . . until, by pure accident, a stray remark made by a passing acquaintance, early on a Monday morning in the fall of 1863, caused him to turn around to his chum in the office . . . and say, 'Ed, I have it—I'll call it the Knights of Pythias.' " Later, he saw a copy of Banim's play and decided to use it as the basis for the ritual of the order.

In the story, Damon has offended Dionysius I, the tyrannical ruler of the Sicilian city of Syracuse, and is about to be executed. When he asks for a few hours of freedom to go and bid farewell to his wife and child, his request is denied. Hearing this, his friend Pythias goes to the ruler and offers to take Damon's place until he returns. Dionysius allows it. Hours later, as Pythias is about to be executed in his friend's place, Damon returns ready to face death. Dionysius is so struck by this demonstration of character and friendship that he sets both men free and begs them to let him be a third party in their firm friendship.

Justus Rathbone finished his final revision of the Knights of Pythias ritual in January 1864 and, at a meeting at Temperance Hall, 914 E Street, NW, in Washington, D.C., on February 19, he read the declaration of principals for his fraternal society:

Justus Henry Rathbone founded the Knights of Pythias in 1864.

"Misfortune, misery and death being written in fearful characters on the broad face of creation, our noble Order was instituted to uplift the fallen; to champion humanity; to be his guide and his refuge, shelter and defense; to soften down the asperities of life; to subdue party spirit; and by the sweet and powerful attractions of the glorious trinity of Friendship, Charity, and Benevolence, to bind in one harmonious brotherhood men of all classes and all opinions.

"The brightest jewels which it garners are the tears of widows and orphans; and its imperative commands are to visit the homes where lacerated hearts are bleeding; to assuage the sufferings of a brother; bury the dead; care for the widow and educate the orphan."

Twelve young men, many of them members, like Rathbone, of a vocal society called the Arion Glee Club, heard him read those words, and, upon taking the oath Rathbone administered, they became the charter members of the Knights of Pythias, an order that would in time become international. Rathbone was elected Worthy Chancellor at that first meeting.

Upon the organization of the Supreme Lodge in 1868, Rathbone was given the title of Founder and Past Supreme Chancellor. At the meeting of the Supreme Lodge in 1877, the year the insurance rank was established, Rathbone was named Supreme Lecturer on the Origin, Rise and Progress of the Order. At the national meeting a year later, he reported that during the year he had visited a great many Pythian lodges across the country, including ones in Indianapolis, Seymour, Covington, and Lafayette in Indiana.

On December 9, 1889, Rathbone died in Lima, Ohio, while on a speaking tour. He is buried beside his wife in Utica, New York, near where he was born. At his funeral service in Lima, Past Supreme Representative Walter B. Richie eulogized Rathbone, saying in part:

"It was because he was human and appreciated the value, worth and need of the friendship of others; because he saw the necessity of charity for the faults of others, because he saw the need of benevolence, that he took the old Grecian story of Damon and Pythias and made every word of it a flower, every line of it a gem, and every page a jewel. He made it so that tonight it is as dear to 250,000 men as the songs our mother sung when we sat at her knee."

CHAPTER 2
AMERICAN CENTRAL

In 1899, while the Endowment Rank was still struggling to survive, an insurance company was founded in Indianapolis that would one day help build on that program the Knights of Pythias had established twenty-two years earlier.

Indianapolis was a thriving city of 170,000 people in 1899. It had an imposing new statehouse, a new county courthouse, and an impressive new Union Station with about 150 trains arriving and departing each day. It could boast of many fine homes, successful businesses, and an abundance of parks and cultural, educational, and charitable institutions.

But the state was far behind others in creating an environment favorable to the growth of private insurance companies. No law required Indiana-based firms to maintain legal reserves sufficient to cover net liabilities on all policies in force. For this reason, many Hoosiers were turning for their life insurance to companies in other states, where laws required the maintenance of such reserves.

Passage of an Indiana Compulsory Deposit Law was obtained on February 10, 1899. It required companies incorporating under it to adopt as high a standard of reserves for the protection of policyholders as was required by any other state in the Union and, in addition, to deposit with the Indiana Insurance Department certain designated securities equal in value to these full reserves. To operate as legal reserve companies, firms already existing in the state had to comply with the law.

Hoosiers could now buy life insurance from Indiana companies with complete faith in the soundness of their investment, and the door was open to the development of nationally prominent insurance firms with home offices in Indiana.

First to incorporate a company under the new law was a group of prominent Indianapolis businessmen led by Elijah B. Martindale. Their company, American Central Life Insurance Company, began business on April 10, 1899, with its home office first at 8 and 10 East Market Street and later in the Lombard Building at 24 East Washington Street.

Officers of the new company, who had been instrumental in getting the Indiana General Assembly to pass the new law, were Elijah Martindale, president; Charles E. Dark, vice president and superintendent of agencies; Lynn B. Martindale, the oldest of Elijah's ten children, secretary-treasurer, and Dr. John M. Kitchen, medical director. Another Martindale son, John T., was later named manager of the industrial and sub-ordinary branch of the company. And among the company's original stockholders were Indianapolis Mayor Thomas Taggart and James Whitcomb Riley, described in the first annual report as "author and publisher."

By December 31, 1900, the company had almost $5 million of insurance in force, with its first policy written on its own vice president, Charles Dark. By 1902, when the company had moved its home office to the Newton Claypool Building, 144 North Pennsylvania Street, it stood first among the forty-four Indiana insurance companies in the ratio of assets to liabilities, and it was lowest in the cost of death claims and expenses. Only four of the forty-four companies did more business in the state the prior year.

In 1902, the company extended its operations outside Indiana, entering Ohio, Illinois, and Missouri. Persons were denied coverage if they engaged in "hazardous occupations," which included felt hat-making, horse shoeing and saloon keeping.

By 1905, when American Central purchased its own building on the northeast corner of East Market Street and Monument Place (now known as Monument Circle), the company had almost $16.5 million of insurance in force and assets of $1.5 million.

The company's investment pattern, which was characteristic of the insurance industry at the time, was to invest its capital and accumulated reserves in highly profitable farm mortgages in the Midwest and later in the far West. This was a pattern that was to continue up to the outbreak of World War I.

Elijah B. Martindale was instrumental in obtaining the passage of the Indiana Compulsory Deposit Law, which requires Indiana-based insurance firms to maintain legal reserves sufficient to cover the net liabilities of policies in force. In 1899, American Central Life Insurance Company was the first to be incorporated under the new law, with Martindale serving as its president until 1904. Hoosier poet James Whitcomb Riley was among the company's original stockholders.

Elijah Martindale retired in 1904 at the age of seventy-six. He was succeeded as president by Addison H. Nordyke, a member of the company's board of directors, who held the office only one year. He was succeeded in 1905 by Milton A. Woollen after a brief but sharp struggle for control of the prospering young company. Interests friendly to Charles Dark had obtained a majority of the company's stock and supported Woollen in his bid for the presidency.

After running a grain and feed business for many years, Woollen in 1893 became one of the principals in an extensive wholesale produce concern, of which he was vice president until 1902. That year he disposed of his interest in the wholesale firm and purchased a large amount of American Central stock. He first became secretary of the company and then was elected president January 4, 1905. He held the office until his death in 1912.

Charles Dark continued as vice president under Woollen, and his activities in the insurance industry in 1904 and 1905 led to his being hailed as the "father of the idea of the American Life Convention."

American Central's policies, in the words of Milton Woollen, "are clearly defined, easily understood, and without trickery in language or intent and the premiums charged are as low as consistent with safety." But the reputation of the industry was being damaged by the actions of some companies. Convinced that the industry should set about putting its house in order, Dark called a meeting in his office in 1904.

He and officers of other insurance companies who met with him recognized the need for an organization that would protect the interests of policyholders and the companies that served them. Out of that meeting, which Woollen also attended, grew the American Life Convention. Today, its

Addison H. Nordyke succeeded Martindale as president of American Central, but he held the office for only a year. Nordyke was a prolific inventor and perhaps his best-remembered design was the racecar that won the first Indianapolis 500 Mile Race, the Marmon Wasp, driven to victory in 1911 by Ray Harroun.

American Central's second home was the Lombard Building at 24 East Washington Street.

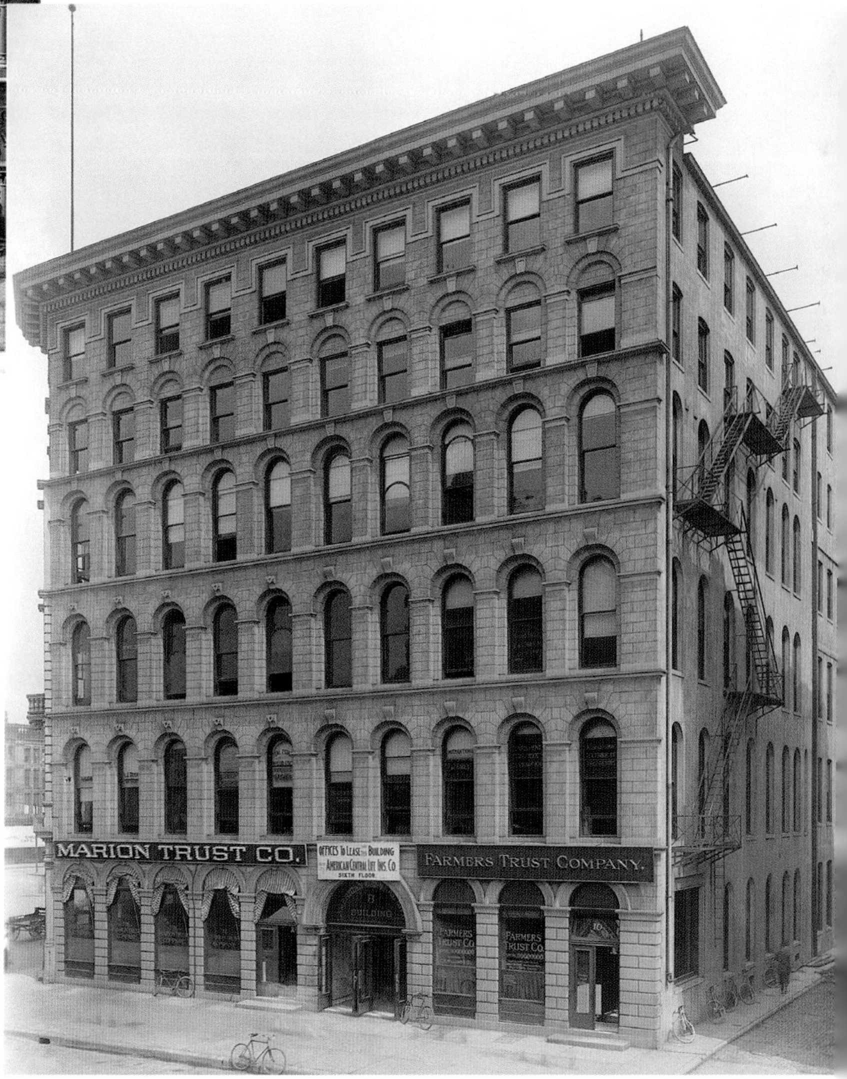

The first home office of American Central was this nondescript building at 8 and 10 East Market Street. The sign over the door read "Offices to lease in this building. Apply to American Central Life Insurance Company, Sixth Floor."

successor, the American Council of Life Insurance, performs those functions for millions of policyholders and hundreds of life insurance companies.

Dark was one of the signers of an invitation to an organizational meeting held in December 1905 in Chicago. Presidents or other executive officers of fourteen legal reserve companies in the central, southern, and western states gathered at the Great Northern Hotel on the day, by coincidence, when President Theodore Roosevelt's message to Congress urged federal regulation of life insurance and railroad rates.

Meeting in evening session, the convention promptly adopted resolutions opposing federal control and endorsing state supervision and favoring "the utmost publicity in the life insurance business." The delegates further invited "the closest supervision of honest public officials" and favored uniformity of laws to "safeguard the interests of policyholders."

A constitution was adopted at a second meeting of the group held in January 1906 in St. Louis. It limited membership to legal reserve life insurance companies, and it listed the purposes of the organization:

"The American Life Convention is organized for the purpose of encouraging, upholding, and maintaining the business of life insurance; the dissemination of information regarding the science of life insurance; the securing of the enactment of uniform laws governing life insurance; the upholding of correct principles in the conduct of the business of life insurance; the establishment and maintenance of confidence between the management of the companies composing the organization and their policyholders; the correction of any abuses which may arise in the methods of transacting the business of life insurance; the promotion of cooperation, acquaintance and exchange of ideas among the executive officers of its membership and any and

Charles E. Dark was the first vice president and superintendent of agencies for American Central and, during his tenure, he made historic contributions to the company and the industry. He was instrumental in founding the American Life Convention, now the American Council of Life Insurance.

all other things incident to the welfare of insurers, insured and the public in relation to the business."

The first annual meeting of the Convention was held in Chicago in September 1906. Charles Dark was unanimously elected its second president, succeeding Joseph B. Reynolds, who declined renomination although he had served less than a year. Dark was described as "an energetic, aggressive, and resourceful businessman, yet a strong believer in the advantages of cooperation among those engaged in the same business."

He was also well aware of the crucial need for cooperation among insurance professionals in 1906 since national attention had been focused on the business by an investigation of its practices undertaken in New York State the previous year.

That investigation was conducted by the New York Legislative Insurance Investigation Committee, which became known as the Armstrong Committee after its chairman, State Senator William W. Armstrong. Its hearings revealed some practices that were questionable, unethical or clearly illegal, and received sensational coverage in the press.

Counsel for the committee was Charles Evans Hughes, who was thrust into national prominence and launched on a long and distinguished public career by the investigation. He later became governor of New York, ran unsuccessfully as a Republican presidential candidate, and finally became Chief Justice of the Supreme Court.

The committee's report, which was published in February 1906, included recommendations for legislation, most of which were enacted in April of that year. Other states were beginning to look at their insurance company activities and the laws that governed them. Among them was Indiana, which realized its system needed revamping.

In November 1906, a Hoosier investigative committee composed of the state auditor, actuary, and attorney general issued a report exposing the weaknesses and inefficiency of the Indiana insurance department and focusing on some of the conditions the committee felt needed reforming.

Indiana had been spending less than $6,000 a year on its insurance department, which was under the state auditor's office. The report recommended establishing a separate department of insurance and banking, with a salary of $5,000 for a superintendent and $4,000 for an actuary. The report charged that extravagant commissions were being paid and, influenced by conservative Eastern advisers, attacked several methods of writing insurance and means of developing Indiana's young companies that were vital to their growth.

Led by Charles Dark, Indiana's twenty-three companies marshaled a surprisingly strong defense. A special examiner from the Kansas insurance department was brought in. He made so powerful a case for the companies' views that, although there was a serious struggle in the legislature, the state left its insurance law practically unchanged.

As a result of the battle, the informal organization of companies Dark had led became, after the legislature adjourned, the Indiana Association of Legal Reserve Life Insurance Companies, patterned after the American Life Convention. American Central was one of the twelve companies present at its first meeting in April 1907.

Milton Woollen capably led American Central through all the turmoil and its aftermath and through the financial panic of 1907. The Armstrong investigation had a long-lasting effect on the insurance industry and its relations with state and local governments. Men in the profession came to speak of eras as "pre" and "post-Armstrong" years, and many agreed with the view that New York's Armstrong laws were a "throttling grip laid upon life insurance in a moment of passing panic."

The 1907 depression was the twentieth the nation had endured since 1790. The sharp drop in the stock market and the series of business failures revealed flaws in the currency and credit structure, which led to the establishment of the National Monetary Company, later to become the Federal Reserve System.

When death claimed Milton Woollen in 1912, his son, Herbert M. Woollen, was elected president of the company, which by then had assets of more than $3 million. Herbert Woollen, a doctor of medicine who was vice

Milton A. Woollen disposed of his interest in an extensive wholesale produce business in 1902 and bought a large amount of American Central stock. He first became secretary of the company and then was elected president in 1905. He held that office until his death in 1912.

Herbert A. Woollen, the son of Milton, became president of American Central upon the death of his father. At the time he took office, at the age of thirty-six, he was the youngest life insurance company president in the United States.

In 1905, American Central moved its home office into a building known as the Fitzgerald Building on the northeast corner of Market Street and Monument Place, now known as Monument Circle. The building, shown in three views in a photograph, a sketch by Frederick Polley, and a painting by Harry Davis, was the company's home for twenty-six years.

president of the company at the time of his father's death, had joined American Central in 1904 as assistant medical director. Dr. Woollen brought with him Indianapolis' first medical secretary, Olive Faulkner. She remained with the company as administrative secretary in the medical department for fifty years, retiring in 1954.

After establishing itself on Monument Circle, American Central produced a company logo featuring the Soldiers and Sailors Monument and the company's new home office. The design has an "American look," a description that could be applied to many of the company's logos over the years.

Herbert Woollen continued American Central's tradition of leadership in the American Life Convention. He was one of the organizers of its medical section and served as Convention president in 1926. In his nomination, he was characterized as "a plain, old-fashioned insurance man of Indiana—capable, diplomatic, successful, straightforward, a patron of the arts, a lover of the beautiful, a modern gentleman of the old school, and a loyal, worthy friend."

In later years, American Central vice president Harry R. Wilson also served as president of the American Life Convention. A boyhood friend of Herbert Woollen's, he had joined the company as a vice president in 1918. He held the same office with American United Life Insurance Company, American Central's successor, when he was elected to the American Life Convention presidency in 1937, making AUL one of the very few companies to supply the Convention with three presidents.

Early in Woollen's administration, American Central displayed its advanced thinking by hiring one of the first female actuaries in the insurance industry. In need of an additional member of its actuarial staff, the company made inquiries at the University of Michigan and found, to its surprise, a woman student was recommended. Helen Clark had pursued her interest in mathematics by studying actuarial science and was to be graduated in 1916. American Central hired her.

Miss Clark's association with the company and its successor lasted forty-four years, ending with her retirement in 1960. In 1942 she was elected to the position of associate actuary in the company, an achievement shared by few women in the industry at the time. Her expertise and professional accomplishments were further recognized in 1950, when she became the first woman to serve on the board of governors of the Society of Actuaries, a position she held for three years.

World War I and then the influenza epidemic of 1918 posed great problems for most of the nation's life insurance companies, and the number of claims paid by many companies for deaths caused by influenza exceeded those paid because of war casualties. Because about one-fourth of the death claims involved relatively new policyholders who had paid only a few premiums, safety reserves were depleted and dividends had to be passed.

In common with other insurers, American Central and the Pythian Insurance Department were hit hard, but they successfully met the combined demands of war and epidemic. The only offset to the heavy claims was the fact that the epidemic did increase the demand for life insurance, and both insurers, which would later become American United Life Insurance Company, wrote an unprecedented number of policies.

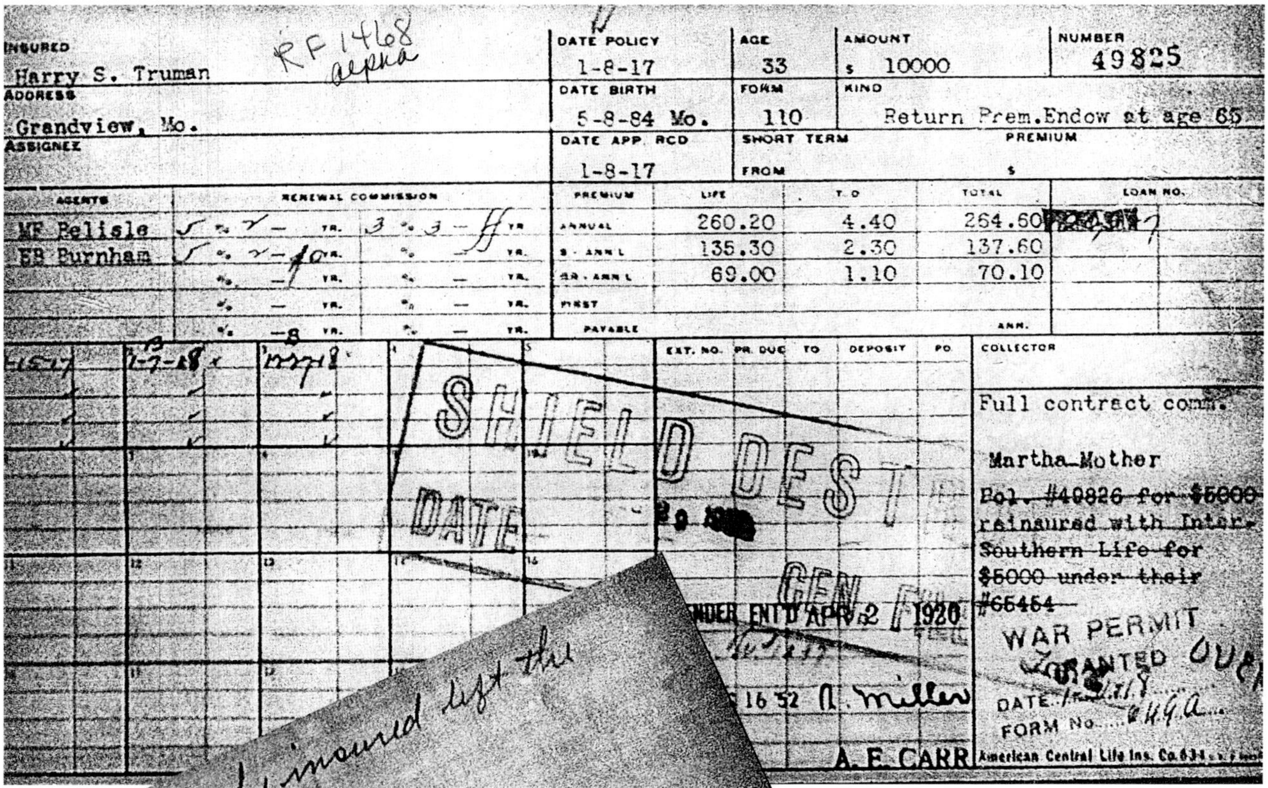

INSURED	DATE POLICY	AGE	AMOUNT	NUMBER
Harry S. Truman RF 1468 alpha	1-8-17	33	$ 10000	49825

ADDRESS	DATE BIRTH	FORM	KIND
Grandview, Mo.	5-8-84 Mo.	110	Return Prem. Endow at age 65

ASSIGNEE	DATE APP. RCD	SHORT TERM	PREMIUM
	1-8-17	FROM	$

AGENTS	PREMIUM	LIFE	T.D	TOTAL	LOAN NO.
MF Belisle	ANNUAL	260.20	4.40	264.60	
EB Burnham	S-ANN'L	135.30	2.30	137.60	
	QR.-ANN'L	69.00	1.10	70.10	

SHIELD DESTR... DATE ... 1920

GEN. F...

UNDER ENT'D APR 2 1920

16 52 A. Miller

A. E. CARR

Full contract comm.

Martha Mother

~~Pol. #49826 for $5000 reinsured with Inter-Southern Life for $5000 under their #65464~~

WAR PERMIT GRANTED OVER...

DATE ...

FORM No. 449a

American Central Life Ins. Co.

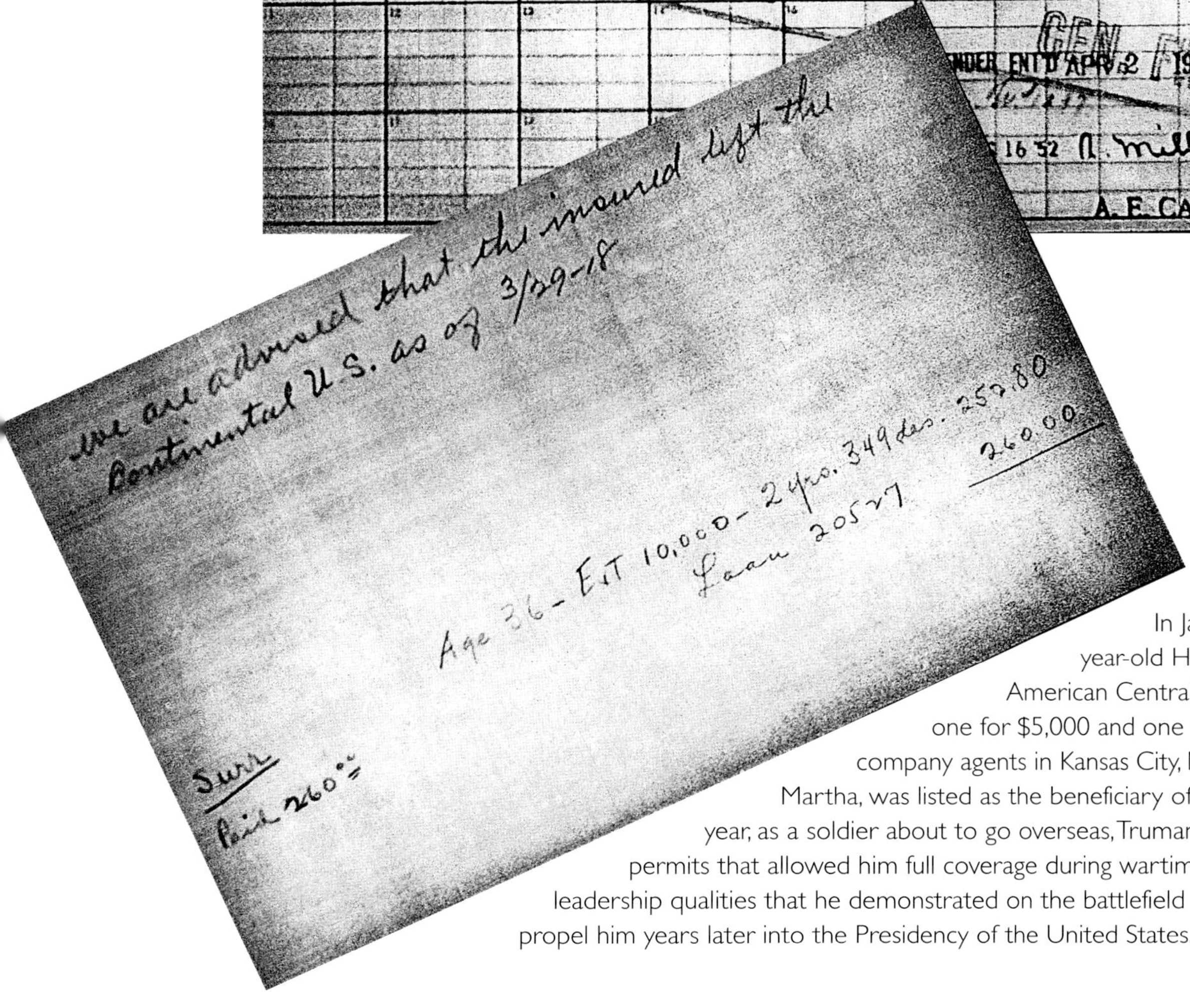

We are advised that the insured left the Continental U.S. as of 3/29-18

Age 36 - Ext 10,000 - 2 yrs. 349 das. 252.80

Loan 20527

260.00

Surr

Paid 260.00

In January 1917, thirty-three-year-old Harry S Truman bought two American Central life insurance policies—one for $5,000 and one for $10,000—from company agents in Kansas City, Missouri. Truman's mother, Martha, was listed as the beneficiary of both policies. The following year, as a soldier about to go overseas, Truman sought and obtained permits that allowed him full coverage during wartime military service. The leadership qualities that he demonstrated on the battlefield in World War I helped propel him years later into the Presidency of the United States.

CHAPTER 3

GOOD TIMES, BAD TIMES, AND NEW BUILDINGS

By the mid-1920s, both American Central and the Pythian Insurance Department were sharing in the general prosperity. Recovering from the heavy wartime and epidemic claims, both of these organizations, which would later combine to form American United Life Insurance Company, could proclaim strong positions and solid assets.

American Central's growth was particularly impressive. The company completed the twenty-first year of its history, 1920, with $100 million of insurance in force. The achievement was celebrated by the unveiling of a bronze commemorative tablet on American Central's twenty-third birthday, April 10, 1922.

The tablet, which was designed and executed by Myra G. Richards, had won the prize for original sculpture design at the 1921 Indiana State Fair. Mrs. Richards described the design as "a triumphant arch . . . upheld by two masculine figures representing insurance, which is supporting a happy family group comprising a mother and her children. At the base of the arch is another group of a mother with two children, neglected and unprotected. The masculine figures are reaching down to the latter figures as if desirous of helping them. The thought of the whole work is 'Protection.'" Within the arch are listed the names of 650 home office and field employees who formed the American Central family at the time the hundred-million-dollar goal was reached.

In 1924 American Central received a great deal of publicity when it sold a $25,000 endowment policy to reigning heavyweight boxing champion Jack Dempsey. The boxer paid the entire premium on the policy, $16,618, that year, and this moved an American Central spokesman to salute his decision.

"This is an act of wisdom on the part of Dempsey," he wrote. "In a financial way a prize fighter's future is very uncertain. [James J.] Jeffries, who made money by the thousands, is today bankrupt, and Jess Willard . . . was in hard financial straits until he came back to fight two battles in New York. . . . Most of them have failed to come back and have died penniless."

Other prominent sports figures followed Dempsey's lead. That same year, American Central recorded the sale of endowment policies to a number of other professional athletes, including Cincinnati Reds star outfielder Eddie Roush, who had just signed a contract that gave him one of baseball's top salaries, $17,000 a year.

The 1922 celebration of a $100 million of insurance in force was small compared with the celebration four years later. The company surpassed the two hundred million mark in the course of a "Hundred Day Drive" that ended on the firm's twenty-seventh birthday anniversary, April 10, 1926. The goal of two hundred million was exceeded by more than half a million dollars, with the final total in force $200,535,591. A cablegram was happily dispatched to President Woollen, who was touring Italy and Spain. It read, simply, WE ARE OVER.

The celebration itself was held during the Memorial Day holiday. More than 150 agents were guests of the company for the 500 Mile Race on May 30, which was won by California driver Frank Lockhart when rain stopped the race at 400 miles. The agents met the following day in the Palm Room of the elegant Claypool Hotel to hear talks by company officers and life insurance experts. A second bronze commemorative tablet, a companion piece to the one placed in the home office in 1922, was unveiled to mark the occasion.

This bronze tablet was erected in American Central's main corridor to commemorate the company's reaching $100 million of life insurance in force, which it did in 1920. Measuring three and a half by five and a half feet, the tablet was designed by Indianapolis sculptor Myra Richards.

In July 1926 the Knights of Pythias Insurance Department moved into this building at 941 North Meridian Street. It required extensive renovation that included doubling the size of the structure and adding a distinctive white terra cotta exterior facing.

The Harry Davis painting of the Knights of Pythias Insurance Department building (right) is part of the AUL art collection.

In the years after World War I, the Insurance Department of the Knights of Pythias followed the pattern of American Central in growing and prospering. Membership in the order rose from 698,890 in 1918 to more than 908,000 in 1921. Insurance in force increased from ninety-six million at the end of the war to $121,000,000 in 1925.

In 1926 the Pythian Insurance Department moved into new offices at 941 North Meridian Street. The former Hassler Shock Absorber and Carburetor Building was doubled in size and a new white terra cotta exterior facing, tastefully decorated with Gothic tracery and motifs, gave the building a distinctive beauty. An unusual feature of the new addition built on the south side was a book vault that rose from the basement to the third floor along most of the south wall. Equipped with an exterior staircase, it offered convenient vault storage for records on every floor.

Retail businesses were to occupy the street floor. The Insurance Department occupied the upper two stories, which were reached through an entrance that combined bronze with green and yellow marble and an ornamental staircase polychromed in blue, yellow, and red.

The third floor housed administrative offices as well as a large workroom, a mahogany-paneled board room, the actuarial department, shipping rooms, and vaults. The office and laboratory of the medical examiner, the library and the publications office were on the second floor, along with the addressing and multigraphic departments, a kitchen, and a lunch room. Later, in 1931, the

The Insurance Press
February 20, 1924

Jack Dempsey's Life Insurance

In commenting upon the purchase of $25,000 endowment life policy and the [...]ment of the entire premium of $16,61[...] Jack Dempsey, the world's fighting cham[...] the American Central Life of Indian[...] has the following to say:

This is an act of wisdom on the part of [...]sey. In a financial way a prize fighter'[...] is very uncertain. James Jeffries, w[...] money by the thousands, is today a bank[...] Jess Willard, Dempsey's immediate p[...] was in hard financial straits until he ca[...] fight two battles in New York. Sull[...] poor man, and Corbett, who spent en[...] in one year to pay for $25,000 of li[...] has very little of this world's goods, [...] reporter on a daily paper. In 15 y[...] will have been forgotten except by [...] older followers of the sport. In fiv[...] have retired from the arena. He [...] out in his next match. When he [...] will soon be forgotten, and his [...] will be gone. He has no other pr[...] unless it is ship building, and that [...] as well as formerly. An old prizefighter [...] followers. Most of them have failed to "come back," and have died penniless.

BASKET BALL PLAYERS SIGN LIFE CONTRACT

With the sale of life insurance c[...] tracts to well-known figures in the [...] letic world stimulated by the rece[...] reported sale to Eddie Roush, [...] player of the Cincinnati Reds, b[...] agent of the American Central [...] a good deal of interest has been [...] in such business. It has been [...] nized that a life contract is one [...] best forms of preserving an [...] income, which is a steady o[...] while he is young and in goo[...] tion.

Probably the most recent sa[...] line is reported by officials of [...] ican Central. John Hurst A[...] company's agent at Franklin [...] policies in that city to Ernes[...] Wagner, coach of the Franklin [...] basket ball team, champions in Ind[...] ana for the last two years, and Robert (Fuzzy) Vandivier, captain of the team. Wagner is believed by many to be the greatest basket ball coach in the country, while Vandivier, according to many critics, tops the list of players.

ROUSH, BASEBALL STAR, BUYS ENDOWMENT POLICY

Realizing the need of capitalizing his present income for use after his days as an athlete are over, and recognizing a twenty-year endowment policy as one of the best means of accomplishing this object, Eddie Roush, star outfielder of the Cincinnati National League baseball club, has taken out a large endowment policy with the American Central Life.

The sale was made by Charles W. Skelton, agent of the company at Princeton, Ind. Roush spends his winters at Oakland City, Ind., a short distance from Princeton. Roush has been in baseball for more than twelve years, and recently signed a contract with the Cincinnati club at a $17,000-a-year salary.

Free advertising! Newspapers snapped up the stories in 1924 when sports figures such as boxer Jack Dempsey and Cincinnati Reds outfielder Eddie Roush bought large policies with American Central.

company purchased the one-story Remington Rand Building south of the original home office for additional space.

Unfortunately, the latter half of the 1920s saw the fraternal system's pattern of prosperity reversed and with it the Pythian Insurance Department, which sold insurance only to lodge members. The primary cause of the decline could be traced to the many changes in the American way of life that dulled the attraction of fraternal orders. The growing demands of business and industry diluted men's attention. The weekly night at the lodge was no longer an automatic prerogative of men. Women were entering the workforce in heretofore unheard of numbers and, after the passage of the Nineteenth Amendment that gave women the right to vote, wives demanded family lives based on equality.

But American Central continued to grow as the twenties progressed, and its attractiveness as an expanding company led to a battle for management control in 1927. The contender for leadership was Arthur Jordan, a former president of Meridian Life and Trust Company in Indianapolis. One of the founding members of the American Life Convention, he had been involved in enterprises that included poultry, pianos and post office lock boxes, as well as life insurance. At his death in 1934, he had been president of three life insurance companies, but he did not succeed in adding American Central to the list.

American Central's home office staff posed for this April 1923 photograph in front of the Soldiers and Sailors Monument.

In a bitter internal struggle, Herbert Woollen proved a formidable adversary. Jordan abandoned his attempt and offered his American Central stock for sale. After reaching a friendly agreement, Jordan sold his stock to industrialist, financier, and philanthropist William G. Irwin, of Columbus, Indiana.

Irwin, who was elected to the American Central board of directors in January 1928 was one of the leaders in a development program then underway for Butler University in Indianapolis. The university was moving from the suburb of Irvington to a new campus in Fairview Park on the city's northwest side, a park that had been laid out by a trolley company to increase its business.

Funds were needed to erect new buildings for the private university, and it was reportedly a proviso of the Jordan-Irwin stock sale that Jordan would donate part of his return to the university. Jordan's contribution made possible the erection of the first classroom-and-office unit when Butler moved to its new campus in 1928. Jordan Hall was named in his honor.

American Central was among the vanguard of companies that, in the later 1920s, recognized the value of advertising, publicity, and public relations. The company sponsored its first radio program in 1926. Broadcast over WCCO, Minneapolis, it dealt with the conservation of health and was preceded by "the actual beating of a human heart" broadcast via "a stethoscope microphone."

Regular use was made of print advertising, and the company published employee periodicals for both the home office and the field staffs. One

newspaper advertisement run in *The Indianapolis Star* might be considered a forerunner of the company's later signboard slogans. It read: "Life insurance is the only thing a man can buy on the installment plan that his wife won't have to finish paying for when he dies!"

Despite the "Black Tuesday" of October 29, 1929, when the collapse of the American stock market signaled the onslaught of the Great Depression, American Central continued with plans to erect an imposing new home for itself in Indianapolis.

President Woollen, on his many tours of Europe during the 1920s, had greatly admired the royal palace in Oslo, Norway. Its classical façade and portico with Ionic columns were the inspiration for the new building planned for the block of Fall Creek Parkway between Illinois and Meridian streets.

The location of the new building was distinctive. It was flanked on the Meridian Street side by the luxurious new Marott Hotel and the Tudor-style Governor's Mansion. On the west, across Illinois Street, stood the large St. Vincent's Hospital. American Central's new home office would look south across a scenic stretch of Fall Creek spanned by two graceful bridges.

Ground was broken in the spring of 1930 for the million-dollar structure, which filled the entire block of the boulevard. Designed by Indianapolis architects Rubush and Hunter, the building was 307 feet long and 52 feet

Field representatives, home office staff members and guests were all in Indianapolis in 1926 to celebrate the company's reaching $200 million of insurance in force.

wide, with three stories in front and four on the Twenty-sixth Street side. It was built of fireproof steel and reinforced concrete with an exterior of Indiana limestone. Construction was handled by the Hunkin-Conkey Construction Company of Cleveland, which had also built the magnificent Scottish Rite Cathedral and the World War Memorial in Indianapolis.

Inside, a bronze vestibule opened into an elegant lobby that joined bronze accents with walls of travertine marble and a floor of Tennessee, travertine and Belgian marble. English oak paneled a large lounge on the upper floor and an adjoining library, as well as the presidential office and boardroom on the middle floor, which boasted a fine built-in console radio. An auditorium with a seating capacity of 350 included a pipe organ rescued from an early motion picture theater. Oak screens and ceiling beams decorated the cafeteria east of the auditorium, and seven large clerical workrooms flanked executive offices in the center of the building.

American Central's new home was dedicated on June 1, 1931, during the annual convention of the company's Field Club. The leading sales representatives attended the 500 Mile Race on May 30 and toured the new building the following day. One reporter described the new building as a "majestic structure of classic architecture . . . in a dignified natural setting."

By the end of the twenties, on the other hand, the future didn't look nearly

American Central broke ground for its new building on Fall Creek Parkway between Meridian and Illinois streets in the spring of 1930. By July the foundation work was well under way.

Exterior construction on the new building was moving quickly by December 1930.

The new American Central Building faced Fall Creek. Constructed with Indiana limestone, the building was designed to resemble the Royal Palace in Oslo, Norway, which Herbert Woollen greatly admired.

as rosy for the Pythian Insurance Department, the other parent of AUL. Along with the changing social conditions that caused the decline in fraternal organizations, disenchantment with fraternal insurance programs had developed, in particular with assessment plans still retained by many fraternal orders. The result was a dramatic drop in lodge membership.

By 1929 membership in the Knights of Pythias had dropped by almost 260,000 from its peak to about 650,000. Because only members of the order could subscribe to its insurance, the Pythian Insurance Department suffered a similar decline in business. From insurance-written income of more than $13 million in 1921, the figure dropped to just below $7 million in 1928, and the average age of members rose more than two years.

It was obvious to both George A. Bangs, chairman of the Pythian Insurance Department's actuarial committee, and the firm of Wolfe and Wolfe, which the Department had continued to retain, that survival depended on separating the insurance activities from the order and making insurance available on a public basis.

The firm's report to the Board of Control in 1929 stated, "The time has come to suggest a change and our recommendation is that the Board of Control consider the advisability of separating the Insurance Department from the order and reincorporating it as a Mutual Legal Reserve Company. This would give the Insurance Department a chance to branch out and make more certain of the fulfillment of its present contracts."

The Knights of Pythias reluctantly faced the economic necessity. It was determined that amendment of the Congressional Charter granted to the order in 1894 was the only practical method of obtaining the separation. Accordingly, a bill to that effect was introduced in the Senate and House of Representatives in the winter of 1929–1930. It was passed by both houses of Congress and signed by President Herbert Hoover on April 12, 1930.

The bill was pushed through Congress by a colorful Republican senator from Indiana, James E. Watson of Rushville. A longtime Pythian, he was assisted in obtaining passage of the bill by another member, Senator Tom Connally of Texas. Watson, who was known as "Uncle Jim," combined a long congressional career with many years of service on the boards of United Mutual Life Insurance Company, the new company, and later American United Life Insurance Company.

The Supreme Lodge approved the separation of the Insurance Department from the lodge and approved the name for the new company at its August 1930 biennial convention in Tampa, Florida. The name, United Mutual Life Insurance Company, was proposed by the Special Committee of the Supreme Lodge that proposed the separation. Immediately after the vote, Bangs and Harry Wade, president of the Insurance Department, traveled to Washington, D.C., where on August 18 papers were filed with the Insurance Commissioner and the Recorder of Deeds, thereby incorporating United Mutual in the District of Columbia.

Above left: American Central's steno pool was photographed in March 1931 when the company was still in its building on Monument Circle.

Above right: The supply department occupied this first-floor space in the building on the Circle.

Left: Roberta Temple Thompkins (at back), American Central's general files manager, kept a close eye on the messenger boys she supervised.

Employees of American Central got this company cafeteria after President Herbert Woollen in 1920 posed the idea to Gertrude Blackwell. In a 1966 interview, Mrs. Blackwell described what happened: "He had in mind a little coffee shop where employees who brought their lunches might have a place to eat and be served hot coffee without charge. He wanted me to be in charge of making and serving this coffee. I was delighted, and we were soon in business with six small white porcelain-topped tables, a water cooler, a coffee urn, electric range, small dishwasher, a hundred-pound icebox, and a little sink. Everyone who brought a lunch was pleased and happy. Then came a day when somebody wanted a sandwich. They didn't expect a free lunch and they would pay for the sandwich. So we gave them ham sandwiches, and Miss Marie Dunn came to help out and serve the sandwiches. By and by, they started calling her 'Ham' Dunn because they tired of ham. So smoked tongue and cheese were added. The next thing we heard was 'Why can't we have a salad of some sort and some soup and maybe pie?' The first thing I knew I couldn't keep up and started yelling for more help, which was provided. There was a switch from cold to hot sandwiches with gravy, then stews, chili, vegetables, and we were on our way."

The new firm's first president was Harry Wade, who had headed the Pythian Insurance Department for the previous fifteen years. Among the members of the first board of directors were Leslie E. Crouch, a Portland, Oregon, lawyer, who was Pythian Supreme Chancellor, and George Bangs.

Wade died suddenly on June 20, 1933, taking with him a wealth of experience and knowledge of the Insurance Department operation. At the October meeting of the board of directors, George Bangs was elected as his successor, accepting the presidency at a salary of $15,000 a year. He closed his law office in North Dakota and moved to Indianapolis, where he would play an important role in the story of United Mutual and its successor, AUL.

Federal legislation in 1932 requiring all insurance companies incorporated in the District of Columbia (as United Mutual was) to maintain their principal offices there necessitated a reincorporation of United Mutual under a newly passed act of the Indiana General Assembly. This was approved on October 16 in a regular meeting of the board of directors, and United Mutual's headquarters remained in Indiana.

It took courage to assume the presidency of an insurance company in 1933. The year before had been the worst of the Great Depression, with the nation's economic system near collapse and millions of families and businesses in dire need.

Economic catastrophe had its inevitable effect on the nation's life insurance companies. Before the end of 1930, sales began a five-year dip that would cause the country's life insurance in force to shrink by $11 billion. Sales in 1932 dipped to new lows and compounded the problems facing insurance companies.

Many Americans were forced to cash in their insurance simply to eke out an existence. Others sought to borrow money on their policies. As bank holidays were declared and laws passed that limited withdrawals to 5 percent of deposits, more and more hard-pressed individuals and businessmen turned to their life insurance companies for loans.

At the same time, investments that had been thought absolutely solid fell victim to the country's economic woes. Many cities and towns were in default on the municipal bonds in which United Mutual had invested heavily. Subsequently, committees formed by the issuers, bond dealers and the banks and insurance companies that owned the bonds refinanced them so that not a penny of the principal invested was lost by United Mutual.

American Central, too, was hard hit by the Great Depression. Its large investment in farm mortgages proved precarious now. Farmers were among those hit first and hardest by the Depression, and defaults in the payment of loan principal and interest increased steadily. In addition, some mortgage loans proved to be less than sound because of incorrect credit reports or inaccurate appraisals.

American Central borrowed $1 million from the federal government's Reconstruction Finance Corporation to help it meet financial demands, particularly those from persons seeking to borrow on their life insurance policies.

In 1932, rather than cut salaries or lay off employees, American Central got all of its directors, officers, and employees to authorize the company to withhold a minimum of 20 percent of their salary each month for use in purchasing some form of personal life insurance or annuity. The type of insurance or annuity was left to each employee. The plan enabled the company to reduce its cash payroll by 20 percent, add to its premium income, increase its insurance in force, and spare its workers a pay cut. It also increased each employee's insurance estate and assured each one a guaranteed cash sinking fund for use in the future. Employees who did not favor a long-term plan could invest in the company's new endowment certificates, which matured in three years and had a guaranteed yield of 8.69 percent.

When United Mutual Life Insurance Company was established in 1930, the company kept the Knights of Pythias knight as an emblem but changed the letters on the shield to convey the new identity.

Insurance companies like American Central and United Mutual were going to every extreme to honor their obligations to their policyholders, paying benefits and making loans as promised. Yet they found themselves being pressed in a legislative vise, as some states passed moratoria on farm mortgages and interest and extended the redemption period for foreclosures. On the federal level, a proposed law would assist troubled cities with new bankruptcy and moratorium laws.

It was small wonder that many insurance executives became disenchanted with the state of affairs. Their income was being cut off by legislatures at the same time that they were being pressed to pay all their obligations. But in 1933, United Mutual and American Central joined with other Indiana insurance companies in getting passage of an emergency bill placing a moratorium on cash loans and surrender values. Passed in March, it was the second of some twenty-six state laws that limited insurance loans and cash surrenders to protect the economic life of the industry.

In the course of the nation's slow and painful emergence from its biggest economic crisis, both predecessors of American United Life Insurance Company were able to meet all their commitments, as were the vast majority of American insurance companies.

One Woman's Story

(The following article was written in 1965 by Eva Woddell McCarthy about her experiences as an employee of American Central and AUL. She retired in 1971.)

After graduation from high school when I was seeking employment in Indianapolis, I heard about the American Central Life Insurance Company and all the advantages its employees had—earned days and bonuses for attendance, good salaries, short working hours, an employees' lunch room, an employees' association which sponsored many worthwhile activities, a summer picnic and fall party every year, and many others. Those were exceptional fringe benefits in those days. Good jobs were scarce then and there was practically no turnover in their personnel. I started working in the office of an office furniture company and became acquainted with Mr. [Harold C.] Pennicke, manager of the personnel department at American Central, who came in occasionally to buy furniture. I was delighted when he asked me if I would like to apply for a job in their stenographic division, and he made an appointment for me to have an interview.

I was interviewed by one of Mr. Pennicke's assistants, a gentleman known as "Cap" Carr. I took a written IQ test. After glancing over my hurriedly completed paper, he said very disgustedly, "I'm sure you could have done better if you had taken more time." I can still see him standing there looking at me over the top of his glasses with a big frown on his face. I passed my typing test 100 percent though, so I got the job.

On July 5, 1927, I started working at American Central in the stenographic division, which was made up of five or six "top-notch" stenographers and a supervisor, also a girl who ran the now obsolete electric typewriters which operated like a player piano, copying the same letter over and over from a roll which looked very much like a player piano roll. I use the word "top-notch" advisedly because if you weren't top-notch, out you went.

For about six months, I went home every evening very much discouraged before I finally began to feel that I might make the grade. We took dictation and typed letters from transcribing machines from every department in the company—agency, policyholders' service, actuarial, advertising, reinsurance, underwriting, investment, legal, and occasionally the president of the company, who had his own secretary. There were many phases and phrases to become acquainted with and every letter had to be perfect before it left the department. Our supervisor made sure of that. The American Central had set rules for spelling, capitalization, punctuation, grammar and letter form, and we followed those rules down to the last comma. Our supervisor counted the lines we typed as she checked our work and our names were posted on a bulletin board each week with the winner at the top of the list, so there was a great deal of competition.

The stenos worked very hard most of the time. We were allowed a fifteen-minute "recess" every morning and afternoon, and these periods of relaxation afforded us a lot of fun. We would stage parties, plays, demonstrations, imitations and all sorts of entertainment—all in fifteen minutes! Our room was at the end of a long hall and one of the girls usually stood guard at the door to warn of approaching trouble.

There are two other survivors of the old stenographic division—Ruth McCord (now Vandivier) and Margaret Ray. Madge Ginn had worked there, but when I started she had already been transferred to Miss [Helen] Clark's office in the actuarial department.

I think the company should have a stenographic department today, to be used as a training school for secretaries.

Shortly before the company moved from its downtown location on Monument Circle to its new building at Fall Creek and Meridian, I was transferred to the agency department. The stenographic division was being gradually disbanded and secretaries placed in the different offices.

In 1932 Mr. Wendell P. Coler came to the company as vice president and actuary, and I was selected to be his secretary. About that same time, I joined a group of ACL employees to take the Life Insurance Institute examinations. We had a study group, and classes were conducted by the different department heads. We studied all about the life insurance business, and the part which was particularly helpful to me in understanding actuarial was learning how, in a general way, to construct a mortality table, compute premium rates and complete an annual convention statement.

In about 1934 Mr. Coler started helping with the bond investment account. It needed special attention because of the losses which had been suffered during the Depression. It was quite a change from actuarial work. I acquired a new vocabulary, words like—"long," "short," "flat," and many others which had a special meaning. Up until that time I didn't know the difference between a stock and a bond. Most of our bond purchases at that time were in railroad bonds so I also learned a little about the railroad business.

The name of the company was changed in 1937 to American United as a result of a merger with another company.

After Mr. Coler's death in 1947, Mr. Frank J. Travers came to take charge of the securities department and more-or-less inherited me as his secretary. I hadn't worked for him very long until I realized it would help me in my work if I knew a little about how to analyze a corporate annual statement, so I took a course in accounting at IU Extension. I also learned by the trial and error system how to help construct a set of wall charts, which Mr. Travers uses to tell our investment story to visitors.

The company began to grow rapidly and we were very busy for several years buying new issues of municipal, utility and industrial bonds, partly as a result of reducing our government bond holdings. This was mostly done by telephone and a great deal of my time was spent helping handle these calls to investment houses. Later we became more active in direct placement loans, which are handled in a different way and do not require so many telephone calls. We also adopted a common stock program, which has always been the most interesting and exciting part of the business to me.

I've been very fortunate in having the opportunity to work for this company, receiving training in the stenographic division, spending some time in the agency department and working for two such outstanding men as Mr. Coler and Mr. Travers, not to speak of participating in the fringe benefits which have been added from time to time.

Eva Woddell McCarthy sits center stage at a meeting of the securities department in 1957 with (from left) Leonard Schutt, Frank Travers, Don Lawhorn, and Jean Hancock.

CHAPTER 4

THE MERGER AND MAKING IT WORK

United Mutual Life Insurance Company emerged from the worst years of the Depression in a relatively good financial position. This was due in part to the fact that a majority of its policies in force were fraternal. That is, while they had paid-up and extended-term insurance non-forfeiture values, they had no cash loan or cash surrender values. United Mutual's commercial policies were too new to have built up significant cash values, so few demands for cash [other than death claims] could be made on the company.

Some cities, counties, and towns defaulted on municipal bond interest owed to United Mutual, but the company was able to maintain its financial strength and retain all its employees. On the other hand, in the mid-1930s, it had really just begun to build a professional, experienced sales force—a significant challenge—and it was still weak in that area. Until 1930 Pythian section officers had been primarily responsible for collecting premiums and acquiring new business for the Endowment Rank.

American Central had a good sales force in the field, and it too had weathered the worst of the Depression. It was not in as sound financial condition, however, and certain of American Central's principal stockholders found themselves in serious financial straits. Herbert Woollen and his close associate, Vice President Harry R. Wilson, had gone heavily in debt in gaining control of the company during the battle with Arthur Jordan. Jordan had purchased about one-third of the company's stock. Preventing him from acquiring enough more to seize control required large expenditures for stock by Woollen and his associates.

American Central began declaring rather large dividends to stockholders in 1927 to enable the owners to clear up their indebtedness. The Depression forced the cessation of these dividends and left the controlling stockholders still in debt. In 1936 Herbert Woollen, who with his immediate associates controlled about 70 percent of the stock, was carrying indebtedness of some $200,000, which was secured by his American Central stock. By that time, correspondence implied that at least some of the creditors were becoming "semi-insistent."

The possibility of a merger between United Mutual and American Central was suggested by Frank J. Haight, president of the Indianapolis actuarial firm of Haight, Davis and Haight and the actuary for United Mutual. Merger talks began in December of 1935.

A merger could produce a reduction in operating expenses by consolidating two home offices and two staffs into one, improve income through consolidation of assets, and give the surviving company more time to develop a new investment program less vulnerable to economic hazards.

Haight's name appears on much of the initial correspondence between the two companies. He provided background material, drew up proposals, and was in constant touch with the principals in the course of the negotiations. Haight expressed his position on a possible merger in a letter to United Mutual President Bangs in June 1936, when he said, "I think this is a wonderful opportunity and we will be making a great mistake if we do not do everything possible to bring it about."

Haight at that time had a twenty-five-year knowledge of American Central and the people connected with it, since he had been employed in the company office at the time American Central's assets first passed the million-dollar mark.

He was able early in the negotiations to describe some factors that favored a merging of the two companies. In a January 1936 letter to United Mutual Board Chairman Alva M. Lumpkin, he said, "The president of the company [Herbert Woollen] is past sixty years of age. His father and mother both died between sixty and sixty-three. He has the same sort of trouble that caused their deaths and feels that he has not long to live. [Woollen lived to the age of 95.]

The merger of United Mutual and American Central merited banner headlines in *The Indianapolis Times* on September 2, 1936.

He has no family except a wife. His inclinations are to spend his summers in northern Michigan and his winters in Bermuda. He wants to retire."

Haight also cited Woollen's reasons for not wishing to sell American Central outright: "To let it become known that the company is for sale would do it an immense amount of damage and it would be impossible to find a satisfactory purchaser without offering it for sale. In addition, there is the matter of personal pride involved. To just sell out would be quite different from merging." Mentioning unscrupulous purchasers who had wrecked insurance companies, he continued: "This makes anyone hesitate about selling a company in which he has a personal pride unless he is very sure with whom he is dealing." Among the reasons he mentioned for American Central's preferring a merger to a sale were the expected larger long-term return and immediate income tax savings.

The nine months of negotiations were conducted in the utmost secrecy. Letters were delivered by hand rather than by mail and were marked "personal" or "confidential." Mention of either company's name was avoided, the initials "A" and "B" being used in their place. Young Harry V. Wade, United Mutual vice president and son of its first president, often served as go-between for Presidents Bangs and Woollen.

A successful consolidation of the two companies posed many problems. American Central was a stock company with a financial obligation to its stockholders, while United Mutual was a mutual company owned by its policyholders (which it appropriately called its policyowners). This difference was resolved by early agreement that the new company would be a mutual in form, although not so called in the new name, and that an exchange or surrender of American Central stock would be arranged. Achieving the latter involved numerous and protracted discussions.

Other questions that had to be resolved included those of personnel, officers of the new company, claims procedures, and the prorating of expenses, profits, and company assets, which included the million-dollar American Central building. The importance of the new company's public image was recognized, and the negotiators agreed that the merger must not suggest any weakness in either company but rather the "consolidation of two exceptionally sound companies for reasons of economy and efficiency."

Lengthy discussions centered on the name of the new company. The suggestion finally adopted was that of Herbert Woollen. When he was interviewed in 1967 at the age of ninety-two, Woollen said, "There were three or four of us in a room talking and everyone had a different idea of what to call the company. They could have wrangled the whole day. But I suggested American United Life Insurance Company." His suggestion had the advantage that only one stone, the one bearing the word "Central," would have be replaced above the entrance to the American Central Life Insurance Company building. Besides, there was already another company using the United American word order.

The merger was the page-one banner story in *The Indianapolis Times* on September 2, 1936, with a headline reading $43,000,000 INSURANCE MERGER LINKS TWO INDIANAPOLIS FIRMS. The article reported that the new company, with combined assets of more than $43 million, would have in force 175,000 policies that exceeded $250 million in value, making it "one of the largest and strongest companies in the Middle West."

Directors of both companies had approved the proposed merger contract on August 31, and the stockholders of American Central were to meet within thirty days to approve the transaction. "The company will operate on the mutual plan," the article went on, "and will sell both participating and non-participating policies." The 850 agents of the two parent companies were to continue "exactly as at present, and all policies of insurance in force will be assumed by the new company exactly as originally written."

Named president of the new company was Herbert Woollen, whose leadership of American Central and American United Life Insurance Company was to total twenty-eight years at his retirement in 1940, the longest tenure of a president in the company's history.

Alva M. Lumpkin, chairman of United Mutual's board of directors, became board chairman of the new company.

George Bangs was named managing director and was charged with the active administration of the company. United Mutual Secretary-Treasurer William A. Jenkins became secretary, and American Central's Henry W. Buttolph, an actuary, became treasurer. Vice presidents of the new company were American Central's Harry R. Wilson, Russell T. Byers, Floyd R. Fisher, and Robert B. Sturtevant and United Mutual's Harry V. Wade and Edward A. Horton. Actuaries were Wendell P. Coler of American Central and Frank J. Haight of United Mutual.

The Articles of Merger were actually signed by Herbert Woollen and George Bangs on December 17, 1936.

Indiana Secretary of State August G. Mueller issued the certificate of merger for the new company on December 31, 1936. It stated that "American Central Life Insurance Company is duly merged into said United Mutual Life Insurance Company and that the name of the latter is duly changed to American United Life Insurance Company," and that "all property, assets and rights of every nature and wherever situated by the non-surviving corporation [American Central] are transferred to and invested in the surviving corporation."

When the merger took effect on January 1,1937, the assets of American Central were $19,303,808 and the assets of United Mutual were $26,460,253, giving American United Life Insurance Company a total of $45,764,061 as it came into being. The total face amount of the new company's insurance in force was $267,767,881, which included $76,215,476 from American Central's direct business, $78,575,463 from American Central's reinsurance business, and $112,976,942 from United Mutual.

The United Mutual workforce moved from the white building at 941 North Meridian Street to American Central's stately and efficiently designed home office building on Fall Creek on Saturday and Sunday, December 26 and 27, 1936, giving up most of a Christmas holiday to follow detailed moving instructions.

The merger, of course, brought with it a multiplicity of changes and adjustments that were unavoidable, and for a few years there was some internal friction as certain problems connected with the merger required mental adjustment on the part of some of the officers from the two parent companies. In time, however, the problems were solved and a more smoothly functioning team of officers and staff was able to devote its full attention to building the new company.

American United Life Insurance Company's investment portfolio was worked over, renewed, and diversified, including for the first time some common stocks, carefully chosen. The field force was enlarged and strengthened, and plans were developed to increase sales.

War broke out in Europe in 1939. France had fallen to Nazi Germany and the Battle of Britain was being fought in the skies over England when Herbert Woollen retired as president of AUL in 1940. George Bangs succeeded him and led the company through the tension-ridden war years.

President Bangs and AUL were saddened in 1941 by the unexpected death of the chairman of the board. Alva Lumpkin, a South Carolina attorney, legislator, and judge, died in August 1941 in Washington, D.C., just ten days after he had qualified as United States senator from South Carolina. He had been appointed some two weeks earlier to complete the unexpired Senate term of James F. Byrnes, who had been appointed by President Franklin Roosevelt

Only one piece of stone over the entrance had to be replaced when the home of American Central Life Insurance Company became the home of American United Life Insurance Company.

to the United States Supreme Court and who was later to serve as Roosevelt's Secretary of State.

Lumpkin had been Supreme Chancellor of the Knights of Pythias from 1928 to 1930. He became chairman of the board of United Mutual in 1930 and occupied the same position with American United Life Insurance Company after the merger. Following his death, Leslie E. Crouch became AUL's board chairman.

Four months after Lumpkin's death, the Japanese bombed the U.S. naval base at Pearl Harbor, drawing the United States into World War II. AUL employees immediately joined other Americans in contributing to the war effort in the armed forces and on the home front. The Employees' Association turned from parties, candlelight dances, and sports to more serious activities. Employees donated blood, saved fat and cans, and planted victory gardens. The association supported food production and conservation with prizes for the best canned beans and the biggest potatoes. Employees were loaned by the company to assist in processing ration books.

Despite the disruptive effects of the war, AUL moved ahead of many other companies in improving employee working conditions and benefits. In 1942, after several years of experiment, a five-day workweek was permanently established. Hours were set at eight A.M. to four-thirty P.M. with a half-hour for lunch; however, employees were free to leave at four o'clock if they were caught up on their responsibilities. This incentive for efficiency allowed many employees to enjoy a thirty-seven-and-a-half-hour workweek. The few who came in on Saturday morning were given compensatory time off during the week.

The next year President Bangs established a wartime policy of paying

Herbert Woollen, who had been president of American Central since 1912, became the first president of American United Life Insurance Company following the merger. He retired in 1940.

drafted employees the difference between their regular salaries and their military pay and promising them a position after completion of their military service. The move drew a complimentary letter from the Indiana attorney general, James E. Emmert, who wrote, ". . . if all employers could do the same thing, it would certainly simplify the problems to arise after the conclusion of war."

In the 1943 annual report, President Bangs reported, "During the war and for some time prior to its beginning . . . the company has attempted to bring into the labor market housewives and others who ordinarily would not seek employment. The company now has forty married women on its payroll." He also pointed out that the company was voluntarily complying with the forty-hour workweek provision of the Wages and Hours Law, even though the insurance industry had not been declared subject to it.

Other employee benefits followed. An employee life insurance plan was established in March of 1944, and a month later the board of directors authorized an employee savings plan.

The company continued to grow, at an understandably moderate rate, during the years of World War II. In 1943 insurance in force totaled $290 million, and President Bangs now reported that the company had been divided into five separate administrative divisions. One handled the continuing fraternal insurance business. The others were responsible for AUL and United Mutual direct business; American Central direct business; business of American Life of Detroit, which had been taken over under a reinsurance contract; and the reinsurance business. Investment activities had been divided into three departments: mortgage loans, real estate, and corporate and municipal bonds.

Leslie E. Crouch, an attorney from Portland, Oregon, and a former Supreme Chancellor of the Knights of Pythias, became chairman of the board of AUL in 1941 after the death of Alva Lumpkin, another attorney and former Supreme Chancellor of the Knights of Pythias. Crouch became president on January 1, 1948, retiring in 1952.

This logo, the first to emphasize the company's partnership philosophy, appeared in the 1950s.

Following the Allied victories in Europe and the Pacific in May and August of 1945, respectively, World War II came to an end. Thousands of servicemen and women returned home and large numbers of them registered in colleges and universities under the G.I. Bill, which paid for a major part of their college education.

At the instigation of President Bangs, AUL established in 1946 an annual $3,000 life insurance scholarship fund to be divided equally between Butler and Indiana universities. It specified that the funds should be used to assist life insurance majors of at least junior standing. The students were to be interested in and qualified for the marketing and service branch of life insurance but were not required to join a life insurance company upon graduation. During its first year of operation, the fund awarded scholarships to fourteen students at IU and seven at Butler.

Eighty-year-old President Bangs announced his retirement the following year because of ill health; it was effective December 31, 1947. He was elected to the newly created position of president emeritus and was succeeded by Board Chairman Leslie E. Crouch, an attorney and former Supreme Chancellor of the Knights of Pythias.

The merger of United Mutual and American Central brought together two very different companies, and the nation was drawn into World War II before the new company could completely overcome the cultural and organizational differences as well as the economic impact of the Depression. But, by the time Leslie Crouch assumed the presidency of AUL on January 1, 1948, the company was well-established and showing strong growth.

Crouch had been elected to the Knights of Pythias Insurance Department board of control in 1928 and had served eighteen years on the boards of United Mutual and American United Life Insurance Company before being elected AUL's president. Therefore, there was no loss of momentum. Within six months, President Crouch had introduced a contributory retirement plan for employees designed to increase their security at retirement age sixty-five.

At the end of 1951, the company's assets had reached $94.9 million—more than double what they had been at the time of the merger fifteen years earlier. The surplus, a fund set aside to protect obligations against emergencies such as wars, epidemics and economic crises, had increased 350 percent to $8 million. And the face amount of insurance in force had increased 80 percent in fifteen years to a new high of $487,383,943.

When Crouch retired as president on March 1, 1952, agreeing to remain on the company's board of directors, he was succeeded by the then-executive vice president of the Indiana State Chamber of Commerce, Clarence A. Jackson.

George A. Bangs

George A. Bangs, who served as president of American United Life Insurance Company in the 1940s, first became involved in the Knights of Pythias insurance program at the turn of the century—or before.

In his autobiography, actually written by his wife, Cyrilla, in 1949, he refers to "more than 55 years of effort and devotion to the upbuilding, development and success of American United Life Insurance Company and its predecessors." So he was probably already familiar with some of the problems when in 1900, at the request of his brother, Tracy Bangs, a leader in the Supreme Lodge of the Knights of Pythias, he "made an investigation and analysis . . . of the affairs of the Endowment Rank."

Four years later, when Tracy was Supreme Chancellor of the Knights of Pythias, a special committee was created to deal with the problems of the insurance program, and the Supreme Lodge formally requested that George Bangs be a part of that five-member committee. He wound up as its chairman.

That committee in its 81-page report to the 1906 Supreme Lodge meeting recommended major changes in the Endowment Rank, including creation of a Fifth Class with four new policy offerings. George Bangs played a prominent role in the debates and discussions that resulted in approval of the committee's report. As a result, Bangs was invited to address the meeting of the National Association of Insurance Commissioners the next year on the subject of fraternal insurance.

Bangs was living and practicing law in Grand Forks, North Dakota, at the time, and, at the request of the state insurance commissioner, he helped prepare and obtain passage of legislation in North Dakota incorporating the insurance reform recommendations of the Armstrong Commission issued in New York State in 1906.

George A. Bangs had been involved with the Knights of Pythias insurance program for many years when in 1933 he was prevailed upon to close his law office in North Dakota and move to Indianapolis to become president of United Mutual.

While still in North Dakota, he served many years on the board of control of the Knights of Pythias Insurance Department. He was chairman of its actuarial committee in 1929 when it became apparent that the Insurance Department should be separated from the lodge and made into a mutual legal reserve life insurance company.

With the help of Harry Wade, president of the Insurance Department, Bangs succeeded in getting the Knights of Pythias to agree to spin off the Insurance Department. He got Congress to amend the law to allow the separation and to allow the mutual legal reserve life insurance corporation to retain all of its fraternal beneficial insurance powers. Then he played a leading role in getting the Supreme Lodge to vote to create the new entity, to be known as United Mutual Life Insurance Company. Finally, he helped set up the new company, including writing its bylaws.

Harry Wade became the first president of United Mutual, and Bangs became a board member. When Wade died unexpectedly in 1933, Bangs finally got into the insurance business full time. He closed his law office in Grand Forks and moved to Indianapolis to become United Mutual's second, and last, president.

When Bangs moved to Indianapolis, he brought with him his extensive law library of more than 7,000 volumes, which he used at United Mutual and later at AUL. He said the vast library was particularly helpful to him and his staff in the rehabilitation of Depression-ravaged securities owned by the company. He also brought to his new position a great reverence for the U.S. Constitution and, at United Mutual and AUL, he saw that special Constitution Day programs were held each year on September 17, the anniversary of the signing of the Constitution.

After Bangs and Herbert Woollen negotiated the merger of United Mutual and American Central in 1936, Woollen became president of the new company and Bangs became managing director, charged with the day-to-day administration of the company. When Woollen retired in 1940, Bangs became president of AUL. He served until health problems forced his retirement in 1947 at the age of eighty. Following his retirement, he was named president emeritus. He died in 1955.

During his lifetime, George Bangs not only distinguished himself as a successful attorney and president of two life insurance companies, but also he gained a great deal of recognition as a polished public speaker, a talent he said he inherited from his father.

Bangs' accomplishments seem even more remarkable considering his lack of formal education. He attended grade school in LeSueur, Minnesota, and one term of high school in Grand Forks. The rest of his education he said came from "the school of experience." He read the law in his father's law offices and, while he never went to college, he often lectured at the University of North Dakota Law School, where his picture was hung in the school's hall of fame.

J. HAROLD THOMPSON

AMERICAN CENTRAL PRESIDENT Herbert Woollen drove a Model A. Ford coupe, "which was a classy thing in those days," recalled J. Harold Thompson, who began working for the company in January 1932. "He also had a radio in his office."

Those were the things that most impressed the nineteen-year-old Thompson, who went to work for the company just a few months after it dedicated its fancy new home office at Fall Creek and Meridian Street. The built-in console radio in the company president's office was just one of many special features of the new building. Indianapolis got its first radio stations just a decade earlier.

Thompson said he was attending business college and working part time at a restaurant in the basement of the Fletcher Trust Building at Market and Pennsylvania streets when he met some American Central employees who ate lunch at the restaurant. At the time, American Central was still in its old building on Monument Circle. Those contacts led to a job offer at a time when few persons of any age were being hired.

"My first job was driving a truck, picking up the mail," Thompson said. "A few months later, I was promoted to the buzz (the internal mail-delivery system). Later, I worked in personnel."

The Depression was still taking its toll in 1932 and the company was still laying people off. "They just happened to have this opening," Thompson said, adding that he began working for fifteen dollars a week but later took a 10 percent pay cut.

In the 1930s, many women didn't think they had an opportunity in business, Thompson said, "but at American Central that was not true." President Woollen, even before the Depression, had hired Olive Faulkner as the company's first medical secretary and Helen Clark, who became associate actuary.

J. Harold Thompson proudly displays his 45-year service award pin.

Thompson recalled a number of other women with whom he worked in those early years of his career, including Louise Henneke, supervisor in the tabulating department; Catherine Harris, supervisor in reinsurance accounting; Marie Eck, supervisor in the billing department; Helen Cox and Edith Snider, supervisors in the mortgage loan department, and Roberta Temple Tompkins, manager of the Buzz and general files.

"Miss Tompkins," he said, "really knew how to crack the whip, but everyone loved her." (Others also remembered Miss Tompkins. One said, "If boys working for her didn't come back from a toilet break as soon as she thought they should, she would go knock on the door of the restroom." Another, who had begun work as a messenger boy, remembered that she would even climb the ladder leading to some storage vaults in search of a messenger boy who might be hiding out there.)

Thompson also remembered that Mary Shepherd and Florence Wilson were working at the company when he was hired. Shepherd was hired in November 1929 and retired in December 1971. She was ninety-five years old and living in Indianapolis when this book went to press. Wilson was hired in August 1926 and retired in August 1970. She lived in Dunedin, Florida, and was ninety-seven years old in 2002.

When American Central and United Mutual merged in 1937, there may have been differences at the executive level, but Thompson said the rank and file at American Central had no problem working with the people from United Mutual. "They were welcomed," he said.

In the reorganization following the merger, Thompson said, the payroll department, where he worked at the time, was moved next to the office of Henry Buttolph, actuary and secretary of the company. Buttolph was a "precise individual and very knowledgeable about life insurance and the company," Thompson said. "Working for that man and rubbing shoulders with him was one of the most valuable experiences I ever had. It was a tremendous help to me."

During World War II, Thompson was in the U.S. Navy from the spring of 1943 until October 1945, and, while he was in the service, AUL paid him a percentage of the difference between his military pay and his company pay. "It was a great thing, I'll tell you," he said. He was also pleased to know that he could have his job back at AUL when he got out of the service.

Thompson said the progressive policies regarding AUL employees who served in World War II may have been adopted because then-AUL President George Bangs had a son who worked at the company. As it turned out, Thompson said, "the son didn't go in, but all of us who did were happy with the policies."

After returning to AUL in 1945, Thompson worked another thirty-two years, retiring in 1977 as senior vice president for administration. Counting his military service, his career with American Central and AUL spanned more than forty-five years.

For Helping the War Effort

American United Life Insurance Company received special recognition twice during World War II for its generous purchases of war bonds to help finance the war effort.

In the Fourth War Loan drive, AUL employees purchased $550,000 in war bonds and won for the company a prize for the largest employee contribution in the district. The prize was a painting entitled *Chimney Peaks and Rhododendra* by Brown County artist Dale Bessire, of Nashville, Indiana. The painting was donated by the Hoosier Salon Patrons Association and the William H. Block Company, an Indianapolis department store.

In what was called the "Mighty Seventh" War Loan drive, AUL topped all competing Indiana corporations with a bid of $10,525,000. This time the prize was the original manuscript of the last newspaper column filed by Hoosier-born war correspondent Ernie Pyle before his death in April 1945. It was presented by *The Indianapolis Times*.

The Ernie Pyle manuscript was presented at Loew's Theater in Indianapolis on Friday evening, July 6, 1945, as part of the ceremony marking the world premiere of the motion picture *The Story of G. I. Joe*. In accepting the manuscript on behalf of AUL, Treasurer Edward M. Karrmann made the following remarks:

> This is not exactly a new experience for us, as our bond buying supremacy in the Fourth War Loan won for us a beautiful oil painting which we were happy to present to Rollins College, a distinguished educational institution at Winter Park, Florida, to be added to their notable art collection.
>
> For the time being, this manuscript will be on display at our company's home office, but I am sure you will be interested and delighted to learn that our board of directors has already decided that this manuscript rightfully belongs with all the other cherished mementos of Ernie Pyle at the memorial now being assembled as a lasting tribute to one of Indiana's best loved and most heroic citizens.

Pyle's column told about B-29 bomber pilot Bill Gifford of Buford, South Carolina, and Gifford's wife was the guest of honor at AUL when the manuscript was presented to Indiana University for inclusion in its Pyle Memorial Room collection. Mrs. Gifford also received a facsimile of the manuscript, which the company had printed in a memorial leaflet that included Ernie Pyle's picture.

CHAPTER 5
The Company with the Partnership Philosophy

From its beginning in 1877, the Knights of Pythias insurance program had always been run by active lodge members. Even when the lodge's Insurance Department became United Mutual, the officers and board members were Pythians with ties that spanned years if not decades.

American Central elected Milton Woollen as its president in 1905, just six years after its founding. For the next thirty-five years, a Woollen ran the company. When Herbert Woollen, Milton's son, retired as president of American United Life Insurance Company in 1940, long-time Pythians George Bangs and then Leslie Crouch succeeded him.

So, the election in 1952 of Clarence Jackson as AUL's president marked the beginning of a new era for the company. Jackson was an outsider. Until he was elected to the board of directors in 1947, he had no direct connection with the company or the men who had been its leaders.

Jackson was executive vice president of the Indiana State Chamber of Commerce from 1939 to 1952. Prior to that, he headed the Gross Income Tax Division and several other agencies in the administration of Indiana Governor Paul V. McNutt. Later, he served as assistant to the administrator of the Federal Security Agency under President Franklin D. Roosevelt.

Jackson was an able administrator noted for his sense of humor. He had grown up in New Castle, Indiana. He knew people all over the state, and people knew him. Persons who worked for him at AUL described him as "a go-getter, a stimulator," as well as "a fun person," and they credited him with "moving the company forward," "getting it off of dead center," and helping get the company better known in the community.

When Jackson arrived at AUL, however, he lacked professional experience in the insurance business. Leslie Crouch and a couple other board members, Frank Dunn and Dwight Carter, were responsible for Jackson's joining the AUL board in 1947. Five years later, when the board convinced him to take the job of president, Jackson said, "I packed two grips and went up in Michigan. When I came back I knew the words of the insurance business—and there are some damn funny ones. They kept telling me this was a non-profit mutual, and I said, 'By God, we better make some profit. I said we must turn around and face competition. Too many people here want to tell instead of sell.' "

The year before becoming president, Clarence Jackson, at President Crouch's behest, had played a principal role in resolving a situation that had demanded a great deal of attention from company executives in the years since the merger. This situation centered around a provision in the merger agreement whereby the former stockholders of American Central had retained, through the year 1956, an 80 percent interest in the new profits emerging from the American Central block of business.

Consolidation and conservation had been the order of the day during the World War II years. After the war, a natural desire to expand the company seemed to be thwarted for several years by the difficulties of making sure that expenditures for growth would not be charged against the American Central share of income on existing business. This was necessary because most of the return from new business expenditures would not develop until after 1956.

This conflict was finally resolved in 1951 by the purchase for about $1 million of all the remaining American Central participation rights, thus accelerating by five years the true completion of the merger. Chief Actuary L. S. Norman, who did the financial projections on which the buy-out was based, said a great deal of time and energy of top executives of the company had been wasted arguing over the allocation of expenses, as between maintenance of existing business and procurement of new business. Thus, with the problem resolved, when Jackson assumed the presidency in 1952, the company was in a position to begin its expansion.

Under Jackson's leadership, AUL introduced in 1954 health and accident insurance as a new product, a step it took after long experience in the more

Clarence Jackson, known for his sharp wit and uninhibited speech, served as president of AUL from 1952 to 1961. He was first elected to the company's board in 1947 and became its chairman in 1957, retaining that position until 1967.

limited field of total disability insurance, which provided waiver-of-premium and disability-income benefits. A year later, the company's group annuities business was expanded into a complete group department with a full line of group life insurance and group annuities.

Formation of the group insurance department was a move designed to meet competition in a rapidly developing field. The expansion was not accomplished without considerable study by the actuaries, who insisted that it be sound, or without some doubts from existing agents as to the salability of group insurance. President Jackson, however, was sure it was a sound step and was among those who termed the 1947 Taft-Hartley Act "practically a mandate for group insurance." He was right. Union leaders quickly recognized the value of such insurance, which previously had been available mostly to white-collar workers. After ten years of operation, the group department could proudly report in 1965 that it had $1 billion of insurance in force.

A longtime leader in reinsurance, AUL expanded its activities in that area also during the 1950s, when million-dollar policies were being sold with increasing frequency to meet various business and estate needs. In the course of the decade, reinsurance was arranged for the first time on a five-million-dollar policy. Expanded supplemental services for reinsurance clients included help in risk selection, both in classifying specific cases and in the preparation of underwriting manuals.

In the early 1950s, AUL adopted the slogan "The Company with the Partnership Philosophy." The slogan, probably coined by Clarence Jackson, was initially applied to reinsurance, but it was soon used to suggest that AUL applies the principles of fraternal brotherhood and sharing to all with whom it does business—clients, policyholders, employees, agents, suppliers, the community, and the insurance industry in general.

In a 1957 memo to top executives, President Clarence Jackson urged broader and more consistent use of the slogan. He wrote:

> I have been getting many letters, and I expect everyone else has, in which a comment is made about our slogan "The Company with the Partnership Philosophy." This was developed when we were working on a new angle of presentation for reinsurance. It has proved very effective. . . . We have been using this now for several years and it looks like we have hit pay dirt. Consequently, we should cash in on it and begin to play it up more.

In 1969, under President Jack Reich, "The Company with the Partnership Philosophy" and the AUL logo became registered trademarks of the company. This action followed a redesign of the company's graphic identifiers during which the popular slogan was given even more prominence than it had before.

In 1956 the company also moved into group reinsurance, a rather new concept. By utilizing AUL's experience and greater risk-bearing capacity,

The still-new group department posed for this picture in 1957. Seated fourth from the left is Sherman Jenson, head of the department. Seated on the arm of the couch, fifth from the right, is Dick Miller, group actuary.

The personnel and services department was responsible for personnel, home office services, corporate minutes, records, and files, along with policy issue, policyholder services, claims, purchasing, and building maintenance. Shown in this 1957 photo are (from left) are Dick Rouch, Lillian Murphy, J. Howard Alltop, corporate secretary and head of the department; Mary Carter; Mildred Galbraith; and J. Harold Thompson, personnel director and assistant secretary.

L. S. Norman, chief actuary (center, in the dark suit) with the actuarial department in 1957.

smaller companies were able to compete effectively for group coverage plans that would otherwise be beyond their means.

Another innovation of the 1950s was the company's student life plan. Developed in 1958, it was tested at the University of Notre Dame and Indiana and Purdue universities. Later it was extended to hundreds of other colleges and universities. Simple term insurance with double conversion rights offered to future business and professional leaders an opportunity to begin a life insurance program at low cost while in school. From initial contacts by mail came many subsequent conversions and additional insurance applications. The successful program remained active until 1968, when the college market became saturated with similar plans.

The expansion of AUL products, which also came to include annuities, pension trusts and group retirement plans, allowed President Jackson to say, "We've got a department store of insurance. We used to sell only to individuals, but now we sell to business firms and partnerships as well. However, the individual is equally important. Insurance is now more for the living than for the beneficiaries."

"Bankers," he added, "tell me it's a dramatic moment when a widow comes in and says she can't finish the payments on this or that because the breadwinner is dead, and they can tell her it's all taken care of."

The diversity developed in AUL's products echoed a pattern of diversity in

In 1961, AUL ran a series of ads in *The Saturday Evening Post*. Under Clarence Jackson's leadership, the company became an active advertiser. This ad was produced by Caldwell, Larkin & Sidener-VanRiper, Inc., AUL's advertising agency at the time and one of the city's oldest ad agencies.

investments the company began in the 1930s. Continuing the practice of including common stocks as a small percentage of its assets, AUL also invested in railroad secondary bonds for a time. It later emphasized industrial securities. The company was among the first to make direct placement loans, beginning in 1947, and spread its investments geographically as well as by type, investing mainly in sound securities, mortgage loans and real estate.

Among the innovations inaugurated under Jackson's leadership were executive workshops for top-echelon officers of insurance companies across the nation. Begun in 1959, these workshops were conducted by the AUL reinsurance department. They dealt with such topics as company management, new developments in the industry, investments, variable annuities, mutual funds and health insurance.

Risk selection and classification seminars were also held for representatives of other insurance companies. These covered the basic principles of home office underwriting and presented new developments in the field. Both seminars were saluted as real and practical contributions to the industry and of particular value to young insurance companies. They were also a great benefit to the reinsurance department, which sought to do business with many of these same companies.

As the fifties progressed, the company grew impressively. New insurance sales increased by 35 percent in 1956 and rose a phenomenal 52 percent in 1957. The face value of insurance in force passed the billion-dollar mark in 1958, having doubled in just six years.

The company's spectacular growth necessitated more space for the activities of its 350 employees, so, in 1957, as it celebrated the eightieth anniversary of its founding as the Pythian insurance program, the cornerstone was laid for a new $2.5 million addition on the north side of the stately home office building. In the cornerstone were placed sample contracts, pamphlets, newspapers, clippings, trade journals, and photographs that related the story of the company's first eighty years.

Speaking at the ceremony, President Jackson said, "American United is a good company. It is good not because it's eighty years old; rather it is old because down through those eighty years it has always been a good company. We who are here today have a responsibility to those who built so well in the past—a responsibility to see that our work and our decisions are sound. Our responsibility is also to those who come after us—a challenge to build well from day to day, so that the yet unknown hundreds, perhaps thousands, of future American United people can well and truthfully say, 'Well done in those early days of the Atomic Age.' "

Behind the home office, the new wing rose five stories high and doubled the company's working space. Designed by the architectural firm of McGuire and Shook, it was a 147-by-98-foot, T-shaped structure in buff brick and Indiana limestone that matched the exterior of the original building.

Besides additional space for departments, a new cafeteria and a medical

At the groundbreaking in 1957 for the first addition to the building are (from left) Clarence Jackson, chairman and president; Frank Dunn, vice president for loans and real estate; Eber Spence, vice president and director of agencies; J. Howard Alltop, secretary; Edward Karrmann, treasurer and controller; and Frank Travers, vice president for securities.

"It was Clarence Jackson's dream," said architect Gilbert Jacobs, who in the 1960s sketched a plan for a high-rise office building on the AUL parking lot on Twenty-sixth Street. Jackson's dream was never realized, but in 1982, AUL moved into a new high-rise office building downtown.

With the 1958 addition to the building, AUL got a new front entrance, facing on Twenty-sixth Street. The five-story addition also doubled the company's working space, and with it came a parking lot for two hundred cars just across Twenty-sixth Street.

laboratory and employee infirmary were included in the addition. Air conditioning was installed in both the old and new sections, and a vertical conveyor in the new wing expedited the transfer of papers. A contemporary entrance and foyer behind a curving driveway faced Twenty-sixth Street, and across the street a block-deep parking lot for two hundred cars was constructed.

❋ ❋ ❋

On January 1, 1959, Mutual Savings Life of St. Louis merged with AUL, bringing the company $16 million more in assets and some $36 million in life insurance in force. Mutual Savings was one of several companies to be merged with AUL or its predecessors. These included American Savings Life of Indianapolis in 1935 and American Life of Detroit in 1939.

American United Life Insurance Company took a giant step toward greater efficiency—and its first step into the computer age—in January 1958 when it became the first insurance company to order the NCR 304 electronic data processing system from the National Cash Register Company. Delivered early in 1960, the computer system occupied almost two thousand square feet of floor space. It was eventually programmed to handle most of the company's direct, reinsurance and accounting functions. In the interim, a smaller computer, the Univac 120, was used to map the programming for the NCR 304's handling of the company's record keeping.

AUL received nationwide publicity in 1959 when it agreed to reinsure

The rapid growth of the company's business required the construction in 1965 of a second addition—this one on the west end of the building. The first of the company's six hundred employees began moving into this addition on May 1, 1966.

The two additions to the Fall Creek building are visible in this view from the northeast. The 1958 addition has the company name on it. The 1966 addition is behind and to the right of the first addition.

policies issued on the lives of the astronauts of Project Mercury. The company's agreement to assume 50 percent of the risk allowed a Norfolk, Virginia, insurance firm to offer the space explorers insurance coverage up to $20,000 at regular rates.

In a letter to the company's president, Jackson said: "Our company is pleased to share with you in offering protection for the families of the patriotic men who have volunteered for the first space trips. . . . As the oldest life reinsurance company, we have pioneered underwriting in numerous extra risk fields . . . we feel that the protection should be provided. Whatever insurance risk may be involved . . . we will assume because of a desire to help and because of our faith in the American way."

AUL was not, however, required to assume what was an unknown risk before the first space flights, as the federal government decided to insure the astronauts itself. The case did cause considerable discussion in insurance circles because there was no experience on which to base expected mortality. The rating offered was explained with the facetious statement that, for men who are departing this world, AUL consulted its "immortality tables."

The year 1960 saw American United Life Insurance Company achieve $1.5 billion of insurance in force and in that category move into the top 3 percent of the nation's 1,440 life insurance companies. A highlight of the year was the sale of a giant group health insurance policy to Indiana Bell Telephone Company. The extraordinary medical expense plan covered between 25,000 and 30,000 persons, protecting them against major medical expense above the level ordinarily covered by health insurance.

A notable event occurred in December 1960 when a man in Texas became the beneficiary of his own insurance policy. Jordan R. Farmer, president of the First National Bank of Richmond, Texas, reached the age of ninety-six and thus outlived the limits of the mortality table in effect when he purchased his policy in 1893 from the Knights of Pythias Endowment Rank. He was presented with a check for $4,120 by the AUL agency manager in Houston.

Clarence Jackson announced his retirement as president in October 1961, saying he would stay on as "chairman of the board and author-in-chief of company signboards." He was succeeded by Senior Vice President Edward M. Karrmann, CLU, a forty-year employee of American Central and AUL. Karrmann took office January 1, 1962.

In the sixties, under President Karrmann, the company continued to set new records. Two billion dollars of life insurance in force was achieved in 1962, the greatest growth year to that time in the company's history. A new record of more than $493 million in new life insurance sold was set that year. Assets reached an all-time high of $184,584,121. Three billion dollars of life insurance in force was reached in 1965, and the asset gain of $15 million that year was the largest in AUL history to that time.

Among the new products introduced in the 1960s were tax-deferred annuities, both personal and group. These made great strides in growth, with benefits under annuity contracts increasing 80 percent in 1964 and 47 percent in 1965.

The year 1966 again saw new highs reached in the company's sales. Insurance in force totaled more than $3.6 billion and new sales of life insurance reached $975 million. Annual premiums for health insurance exceeded $10 million, and annual retirement benefits under outstanding annuity contracts topped $15 million.

This significant year-after-year growth was the achievement of a field force that was unusually enterprising. In 1966, a company record 112 AUL career agents received the National Quality Award for sales and service to clients. The number of agents who, through study and training, had achieved the designation of Chartered Life Underwriter (CLU) placed AUL in the top 3 percent of the nation's insurance companies in that category. The youngest person ever elected president of the Million Dollar Round Table, an association of the world's top-echelon life insurance salesmen, was forty-two-year-old Frank E. Sullivan, CLU, AUL's agency manager in South Bend, Indiana, who was elected in 1966.

The company's unprecedented growth demanded the addition of a second wing to the home office in 1965. Ground was broken on February 22 for a five-story, $2 million structure that would add 77,000 square feet of space to the older portions of the building. Increasing usable working space by 70 percent, it extended north along Illinois Street from the original building and matched the older section in design and exterior facing. The first of the company's six hundred employees moved into the second addition in May 1966, and by November it was in full use. The addition included a new cafeteria and meeting/dining rooms on the fourth floor and allowed the

Edward M. Karrmann, CLU, AUL's president from 1962 to 1968, worked at American Central every summer of his college career at Indiana University. Upon graduation in 1925, he accepted a full-time position in the actuarial department, which began a forty-three-year career with the company. During that career, he twice served as president of the Insurance Accounting and Statistical Association. He also served on the board of the Life Office Management Association (LOMA) and wrote a textbook, *Life Insurance Record-keeping and Accounting*, used by the LOMA Institute.

location of related departments close to one another, which speeded the handling of AUL's ever expanding business.

The company's spectacular growth continued in 1967, with life insurance in force reaching $4 billion and, for the first time in company history, the face value of new business for the year exceeded $1 billion. Assets reached a new high of $265 million, and the company's surplus was nearly $20 million. AUL showed the largest percentage gain in premium income over the prior ten years of any of the nation's top fifty mutual companies.

When Clarence Jackson resigned as chairman of the board, Jack E. Reich was chosen to succeed him at a special meeting on October 18, 1967. Reich, chairman of the board and chief executive officer of the Indianapolis Water Company, was also named chief executive officer of AUL at the meeting. He had been an AUL board member since 1957 and chairman of the executive committee since February 1967. Jackson retained his membership on the board.

In 1967 the board established a policy of automatic retirement at age sixty-five, forcing President Karrmann to retire on July 1, 1968, completing a forty-three-year association with AUL and its predecessor, American Central. The company's annual report that year paid tribute to his dedicated career, saying his "effective leadership has been a constant source of inspiration" to company personnel and throughout the insurance industry. He had twice served as president of the Insurance Accounting and Statistical Association. He was named an honorary member of the AUL board of directors. And Jack Reich, who was already the company's chairman and chief executive officer, was given the additional title of president.

AUL celebrated its ninetieth anniversary in 1967 with the news that it had reached $4 billion of life insurance in force.

This group of AUL employees sang carols throughout the building prior to Christmas 1965. In the 1960s, wing parties, as they were called, were held in many parts of the building at Christmastime. Stories about some of the goings-on at those parties circulated among employees for years afterward.

L. S. NORMAN

L. S. NORMAN WENT to the University of Michigan to study architecture. At least, that is what his mother wanted him to do. But after discovering actuarial science and seeing a display on Michigan actuarial science graduates who had become top officers of insurance companies, he changed his major.

Norman had entered school in the fall of 1929 with only $200 of borrowed money, but he found work at a nearby fraternity house and at the university library. And thus paying his own way through school, he earned a bachelor's degree in 1935 and a master's in business administration in 1937.

Upon graduation, he landed a job as an actuarial assistant at Central Life Insurance Company of Illinois. In 1941 he became actuary of Michigan Life Insurance Company in Detroit. When he joined the navy in 1943, his talents landed him a commission, the rank of lieutenant junior grade, and an assignment to the newly formed Aviation Planning Division of the Navy Department in Washington, D.C. There he played an important role in strategically projecting the future requirements and availability of various types of naval aircraft. These were key numbers for the integrated aeronautic program promulgated by Admiral Arthur Radford.

Following his discharge from the service in October 1946, he became an assistant actuary at Guarantee Mutual Life Company in Omaha, and that is where American United Life Insurance Company found him in 1949. A year later, he finished his actuarial exams and became a Fellow of the Society of Actuaries (FSA), and that same year, following the death of Actuary Frank Haight, he became AUL's chief actuary.

L. S. Norman retired in 1977 as senior vice president of the company. At that time, he was the second ranking executive in the company as well as a member of AUL's board of directors and its executive committee.

L. S. Norman

In a tribute to Norman at his retirement, Dr. John Pearson, vice president for medical and underwriting, said, "I would bet even money that [his] files contain material pertinent to every major policy decision made in almost every department in the company.

"Many actuaries are specialists, but many of us consider Norm as a specialist in many specialties—product preparation and pricing, public relations, agency compensation, underwriting, taxation, legal ramifications, data processing, and you name it. He has been American United Life's Mr. Insurance."

In the last few years of his working career, Norman also gained a reputation as a specialist in quips for the AUL signboards. His personal favorite was "Procrastinate Now," but he got his reputation for more controversial ones, such as "My wife is outspoken, but not by many," and "To be an atheist is a God-given right." That last one caused such a storm of protest from a few people who lacked a God-given sense of humor that it stayed on the boards less than one day.

THE PEOPLE BEHIND THE SIGN

THE AUL SIGNBOARDS appeared originally in 1958 with apologies for the inconveniences caused by construction of an addition to the home office on Fall Creek Parkway. They remained to become company landmarks.

When the construction was completed, up went a line boasting that AUL had—OVER A BILLION DOLLARS OF INSURANCE IN FORCE. The next week the company wished passersby a happy Thanksgiving. Then motorists were reminded to drive safely over the holidays.

With the new year came the first humorous quip: WHAT THIS COUNTRY NEEDS IS A GOOD FIVE-CENT NICKEL. The next week the signboards were again sermonizing about safe driving but this time with tongue in cheek: AVOID THAT RUNDOWN FEELING—OBEY STOP SIGNS.

The genius behind the signboards was Clarence Jackson, AUL's president from 1952 to 1961 and a man with a keen eye for humor. Many of the early sayings were his own, and he reviewed suggestions from employees and the public, nixing those that might offend people or that were, as he put it, "too preachy."

Very soon, the company began offering five dollars and a miniature replica of a signboard with the contributor's quip on it for every suggestion that was used. That is still the policy.

In the 1970s, before it moved into its distinctive, thirty-eight-story office tower downtown, AUL was best known to many Indianapolis residents as "the company with the signboards." And for a time its advertising capitalized on this popularity by inviting potential customers to "put the people behind the sign behind you."

Trends in signboard subjects began to develop early. Popular topics such as money and finances, marriage, cars, kids and the weather dominated the suggestion lists. Puns and plays on words were common. But there have been changes too. For years, AUL got laughs with quips about women: GENERALLY SPEAKING, WOMEN ARE. WOMEN LIKE THE SIMPLE THINGS IN LIFE—MEN. And, GIVE A WOMAN AN INCH AND SHE WILL RE-DECORATE IT.

Today the company is very sensitive to quips that might offend some group or organization, but still there

A single signboard was located at Fall Creek Parkway and Illinois Street. This is an early version of the signboard, which was redesigned in 1969 when a new AUL logo was adopted.

Two signboards stood at the corner of Fall Creek Parkway and Meridian Street.

This was the last quip posted at the Fall Creek location before the company moved downtown in October 1982.

are occasional complaints. Judging what is funny and not offensive to anyone is a tricky business. No one expected complaints about WHEN THE CHIPS ARE DOWN, THE BUFFALO MOVE ON, but that quip survived only a day or two on the signboards.

Then there is the quip that made news: TO BE AN ATHEIST IS A GOD-GIVEN RIGHT. Within hours of the time that line appeared on the signboards, a woman was in the AUL lobby to complain. A little later the phone calls began. The quip was taken down before the end of the day. But there was still a problem.

Radio newsman Fred Heckman had seen the quip while it was up. He liked it and used it in his "My Town Indy" feature on WIBC. People heard him mention it, and they looked for it as they passed AUL—except the quip was no longer there. Heckman got calls. He called AUL. Then he did another column to explain what happened.

The genie was out of the bottle. *The Indianapolis Star* heard about the flap and ran a news story on it. A day or two later, it ran an editorial. The calls and the letters to AUL and the newspaper went on for several more days. Later that summer, the Reverend Richard Hamilton of North United Methodist Church wrote a column in his church's newsletter in which he said it is a sad commentary when the most serious theological debate of the summer is sparked by an insurance company signboard.

Because so many people have asked about the signboards, AUL has published a booklet of signboard quips, which has been updated on several occasions. Newspaper, radio, and television reporters have done a number of stories on the popular signboards, and the signboards would probably not exist today if it were not for one of those stories.

When AUL was building its new building downtown, David Mannweiler, then with *The Indianapolis News*, called and asked if the company would keep the signboards when it moved downtown. He was told "probably not," since the architects said they would detract from the appearance of the new building. He wrote a story to that effect, and the calls and letters started coming again. People wanted AUL to keep the signboards. Mannweiler did a second story. AUL got the message and figured out a way to put the signboards on two corners of its employee parking lot downtown, where they stand today—more than forty-three years after being erected as temporary signs at a construction site.

Few quips are used more than once, but this greeting has appeared on late-December signboards for many years.

This heartfelt message appeared on the downtown signboards following the terrorists' attack of September 11, 2001.

CHAPTER 6

FORTUNE BOUND

Jack Reich was an executive like Clarence Jackson in many ways. Not blessed with a silver tongue or oratorical wit as Jackson was, Reich was, nonetheless, a tough-minded, intelligent organizer with superlative management skills—and plenty of business experience. And he believed a mutual life insurance company should be run like any other business, and it should make a profit as needed to finance continuing growth.

In the depths of the Great Depression, Reich wangled a job in state government and went to work for Clarence Jackson, who ran the newly created Gross Income Tax Department. At first, Jackson didn't want him and threatened to have him fired, but, in time, Reich proved his worth and became a supervisor of older, more experienced men. Jackson became Reich's mentor.

When Jackson became executive director of the Indiana State Chamber of Commerce, he hired Reich. When he left that position to become president of AUL, he made sure that Reich moved up to succeed him. John Barnett, who also worked at the State Chamber and who followed Reich as executive director there, said Bill Book, who headed the Indianapolis Chamber of Commerce at the time, was expected to get the top job at the State Chamber. When Jackson found that out, Barnett said, Jackson got on the telephone and waged a campaign that got the job for Reich. A few years later, he brought Reich on the AUL board of directors, and, when Jackson retired as board chairman, Reich was once again his handpicked replacement.

"AUL was kind of a sleepy little company when Jackson went there," Barnett said, "and I think he turned it around, activated the place, and I think Jack carried on what Jackson started." Harold Ingersoll, a former AUL board member, said Jackson was the one "who brought business methodology into the corporation." He said Reich "took it from there and just kept pushing it right on and on," adding that Reich had outstanding skill as a business manager.

Jack Reich was the first person at AUL to be given the title of chief executive officer, and at a meeting of home office employees soon after his election as chairman and CEO in October 1967, he kicked off a campaign to build the company's assets and its prestige. He called it "Fortune Bound."

In a specific sense, he wanted to see AUL listed by *Fortune* magazine in its "Top Fifty Life Insurance Companies," ranked by assets. More generally, he said, the good fortune of the company means good fortune for its employees in the home office as well as in the field. If each person is fortune bound, then the company will be too.

"American United Life's home office and field personnel are associated with a company that believes in its employees and their ability to get the job done," Reich said. "The good fortune of association has been a strong force enabling AUL to increase its insurance in force eightfold in the past fifteen short, but very exciting, years.

"This is a 'partnership philosophy' project, with the field force and home office staff combined in a total effort to build and conserve assets. The sales and office staffs each will play a major part. Let's be fortune bound together. It is no accident that American United Life is one of the top insurance companies in the United States. Sound execution of each individual's job will make AUL indeed Fortune Bound!"

At the end of 1967, AUL, with assets of $265 million, was twenty places away from being in *Fortune*'s list of the fifty largest life insurance companies in the United States, but AUL succeeded in making the list for the first time in 1976. That year, based on 1975 asset totals, AUL was the forty-ninth largest life insurance company in the nation. In subsequent years it moved as high as forty-fourth before dropping back.

Soon after kicking off his Fortune Bound campaign, Reich created a marketing committee on the board of directors to explore new product research and design and marketing procedures.

In 1969, Reich reorganized the administrative structure of the home office, creating three divisions—marketing, insurance and administration. The marketing division was comprised of direct insurance sales, research, devel-

Jack E. Reich was elected chairman and chief executive officer of AUL in 1967 when Clarence Jackson retired from the board. Reich was the first person at AUL to be given the title of chief executive officer. He was given the added title of president in 1968 following the retirement of Edward M. Karrmann.

opment, and the departments of accident/health and group/pensions. The insurance division included actuarial, underwriting, medical, policy issue and reissue. The administration division covered electronic data processing, policy title, benefits, claims, and policy accounting.

In addition, with the help of Senior Vice President L. S. Norman, Reich designed and implemented for employees what he called a Progress Sharing Plan. Under the plan, employees with the company more than two full calendar years qualified to participate. Each year participants were to share in the company's progress based on (1) net gain from operations, (2) growth in premium income, and (3) a measure of how well the company controlled expenses. The money was to be invested in a high-grade equity fund maintained by the company, and employees would get their shares when they retired or left the company.

The first year, 380 employees qualified for bonuses equal to 1.72 percent of their annual income. By 1972 there were 413 eligible employees and the Progress Sharing bonus for that year was 5.57 percent.

The company in 1969 also developed a new corporate identity program and registered as trademarks the AUL logotype and the slogan "The Company with the Partnership Philosophy." The slogan had been in use since the early 1950s; now it was being emphasized. At the same time, a rule in the new standards said: "American United, which is often used, is not considered compatible with our AUL logo so the briefest form (of the company name) we may use is American United Life." It was felt that the use of the AUL logo as a company identifier would help the company distinguish itself from the many insurance companies whose names began with "American."

That same year the company entered the equity products field, establishing a subsidiary sales and service organization. AUL Equity Sales Corporation was a registered broker dealership that sold various mutual funds. AUL sales representatives also began offering group and individual variable annuities for qualified pension plans.

The ochre color and the Torino typeface gave AUL's logo a clean, modern—and distinctive—look when introduced in 1969.

In 1970 another subsidiary, Affiliated Services Corporation, was founded for the mass marketing of life insurance and mutual funds through payroll deduction. That operation was later dropped.

The company continued its practice of conducting workshops for fellow members of the industry, including executive workshops on industry issues, underwriting workshops, and estate-planning seminars conducted by representatives of the fields of law, finance and insurance.

The industry was rapidly becoming a more complex and competitive business with many new products and variations and with sophisticated marketing techniques. In addition, the early 1970s were marked by an economic recession. But AUL continued to do well. The goal of $5 billion of life insurance in force was reached in 1970, and assets climbed to $355 million.

In 1969 and 1970, AUL made $1 million in loans to residential borrowers in Indianapolis' inner city, fulfilling its commitment to a billion-dollar urban investment program developed by the Institute of Life Insurance.

Life insurance in force passed the $6 billion mark in 1972, and the next year assets rose above the $500 million mark. The company reached $7 billion of life insurance in force on September 30, 1974, and the company's net gain from operations set a record high of $5.4 million. The following year assets increased $99 million to $678 million and, on the basis of that achievement, AUL made *Fortune* magazine's 1976 listing of the Fifty Largest Life Insurance Companies in the United States.

In 1975 the company allocated a record total of $12.8 million in policyowner dividends. This figure reflected the largest single increase, an average of 7.7 percent, ever granted by the company in dividend rates for personal life insurance.

One cause for the impressive, steady growth of AUL through the early 1970s was the continuing improvement of its products and expansion of its coverage. In 1973 AUL introduced an exciting and totally new concept in the field of disability and income insurance called income replacement insurance. It recognized that the loss of earnings was the true loss in the case of partial or complete disability due to sickness or injury, and it paid benefits whenever earnings fell below 80 percent of the insured's normal income. The monthly benefit was 80 percent of the individual's average earnings less any net income during the month, subject to the maximum monthly benefit purchased.

The income replacement policy was enthusiastically received by both the public and the industry. It drew praise from a competitor in 1975 when, at a Health Insurance Association of American seminar, the vice president of another life insurance company said, "I credit American United Life for its pure income approach, which does relate benefits to income at all stages. . . . Personally, I would like to see the pure income coverage of American United Life developed."

Also made available in 1973 was a new yearly renewable term policy of life insurance. It was a low-cost participating policy that was convertible and could be renewed every year up to age seventy. Dividends were payable beginning at the end of the third policy year. In 1974 new benefits were added to the series of disability income policies introduced the year before. Introduced in 1975 was the Family Security Plan, a series of low-cost ordinary life insurance policies that was offered to employer-employee groups on a payroll-deduction basis. That same year, a new group product of individual retirement annuities was developed. The contracts, called Group Pension Builders, closely resembled the policies offered in the tax-deferred annuity market, which the company had entered in 1963.

Another innovation introduced in 1975 was AUL's "ten-day free look," offered to all purchasers of life insurance or deferred annuity policies. This privilege of a leisurely examination of a new policy, which had been part of health insurance policies for several years, allowed the buyer to return a policy within ten days if he or she was not satisfied with its provisions and receive a refund of any premium paid.

In January 1976, the company's board of directors voted to add to the proceeds of policies any interest earned during the period that might be required to complete settlement following the death of an insured or the maturity of a policy. That year the company also made improvements, in anticipation of new pension legislation, in retirement plan sales and service programs for both corporations and individuals.

In addition to new and improved products, the company's success was greatly aided by operating innovations, most notably in electronic data processing. In 1969, AUL supplemented the NCR 304 with a rented IBM 360 Model 40 computer and began to adopt the Advanced Life Insurance System (ALIS) programming package that greatly improved service to policyowners

F. Leslie Barlet was elected president of AUL in 1977. He had been with the company for thirty-six years and was serving as senior vice president for administration and corporate finance when he was elected president. Reich continued as chairman and chief executive officer.

and agents. The change to computerized accounting was completed by January of 1974, and despite some frustration in moving from manual to computerized operation, the switch eventually produced great improvements in accuracy and efficiency. The first IBM mainframe computer was quickly replaced by a second, third, and then fourth as technology improved computer capacity and speed. The venerable NCR 304 was finally retired at the end of 1976 when it was sold for parts to the American Greeting Card Company.

In 1973 a word-processing department was established to streamline and speed the production of the company's written communications through the combined use of systems management procedures, computer technology, and trained personnel. That same year, the company began microfilming its thousands and thousands of records. Some accounting records were the first to be put on film, with 315,000 active policies to follow.

In March 1973 Jack Reich announced improvements in employee retirement benefits. Monthly benefits were increased and early retirement was made more attractive. The new plan also provided a guaranteed life income for the surviving spouse of an employee who had attained age fifty-five and had ten years' service with the company. That same year, employees began receiving nine paid holidays a year, an increase of two and a half.

In 1974 the company paid its first million-dollar death claim. It paid on two $500,000 policies on the life of a New Jersey corporation president who died following an automobile accident. The company had previously paid portions of million-dollar death claims through its reinsurance division.

That year also computer technology began to become available in product departments. First, the pension department purchased a complete computer system to assist in preparing proposals and provide administration for its sales

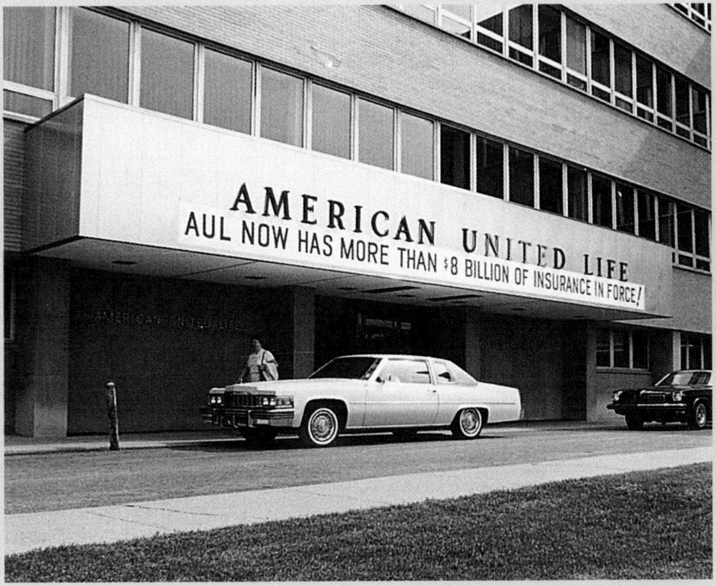

Early in 1977 the company announced that the face amount of its life insurance in force exceeded $8 billion, double what it had been a decade earlier.

force. The next year the group department installed a Wang computer to speed the issuing of group proposals and improve the accuracy of group rate calculations.

Improvements in the compensation plan for general and career agents were made in July 1975, the first basic changes in compensation for the field force in nearly thirty years. Increases in compensation were accompanied by improved fringe benefits. The plan also incorporated a new assistant general agents' program and a financing program designed to produce new general agents from within the AUL field force.

In the spring of 1976, Chairman Jack Reich held a briefing for all home office employees, the first of what became an annual event. It was a presentation similar to one he did for the board of directors, reviewing the results of the past year and talking about the company's goals for the present year.

"While we like to be big, we are more concerned about being a strong company," he told the employees, adding that, while AUL is a mutual company, it is still important to make a profit. He also urged employees to give good service to policyowners and to "be patient and helpful" in working with members of the field force, who, he said, "are out there all alone, and they don't get paid unless they make the sale."

When Clarence Jackson died later that year, Reich paid special tribute to him. "Clarence Jackson really put a spark of life into AUL back in 1952," he said. "With his ability to plan, to organize and to motivate people, he gave the company outstanding leadership. In addition, he did a lot of good things for people, many of whom never knew it was he who helped them."

The company's hundredth year—1977—proved to be a memorable one. In February, the board of directors nominated and the policyowners elected AUL's first woman director, Freda Lockhart, chairman of the board of Cleverly-Lockhart Cadillac in Indianapolis. In April Reich decided to share his management responsibilities and the board of directors named F. Leslie Barlet as president. Reich remained as chairman and chief executive officer. Barlet, who had been with AUL since 1941, was senior vice president of administration and corporate finance.

On November 6, 1976, AUL employees rang in the company's centennial year with a gala dinner-dance at the Marott Hotel across Meridian Street from the home office. As the hour of midnight struck, employees ushered in the company's hundredth year with noisemakers, horns, and the cutting of a five-tiered birthday cake. (As historical research now indicates, the Knights of Pythias insurance program was started in November 1877, but there is no evidence showing the actual birthday to be November 7.)

On November 6, 1977, AUL employees, agents, directors, retirees, and friends of the company joined in a big centennial celebration at Clowes Hall on the Butler University campus. About fifteen hundred persons attended.

Reich, speaking at the special ceremonies, called the big event, "A most fitting salute to a company that has weathered all the storms and met all the

AUL® WE HAVE BEEN GUARANTEEING FUTURES FOR 100 YEARS

PUT THE PEOPLE BEHIND THE SIGN BEHIND YOU

ɔday, we at American United Life Insurance Company are celebrating e 100th anniversary of our company. We started in November, 1877, ıd today, AUL has a million and a half policyowners in all walks of life. ıe company writes all forms of individual life and health insurance and sability income policies, plus group life and health insurance, tax-ferred annuities, individual retirement accounts and pensions. It is also volved in the sale of mutual funds and mass-marketed insurance prod-ts, as well as ranking among the national leaders in the specialized ld of reinsurance.

ɔday, the company has $900 million in assets and has earned a place on Fortune Magazine's listing of the 50 largest life insurance companies in the United States. Insurance in force totals more than $8.3 billion.

Today, AUL's highly trained sales force is licensed to operate in 40 states and the District of Columbia. And now more than 630 of us work in the company's home office at Fall Creek and Meridian, right behind those signboards with the humorous quips.

We at American United Life are telling you all of this because we are proud of the fact that our company has been guaranteeing futures for 100 years.

AUL® Guaranteeing futures for 100 years

American United Life · One West 26th Street · Indianapolis

Many of the "people behind the sign" are included in this ad that ran in *The Indianapolis Star* on Monday, November 7, 1977. Jack Reich is in the center of the front row. The ad was produced and placed by Lacy Advertising, an agency headed by Richard Lacy, an AUL vice president from 1970 to 1974.

challenges of a century and emerged with a firm commitment to the future. . . . When we say 'we have been guaranteeing futures for 100 years' [a company slogan at the time], we intend to convey not only a pride in our company's past accomplishments, but also a strong desire to continue serving people in the years to come."

The Hoosier Heritage Award, created by the State Department of Commerce to recognize 100-year-old Indiana-based companies, was presented to AUL at the celebration by Donald Moreau, executive director of the Indiana Department of Commerce. Indianapolis Mayor William H. Hudnut III read a proclamation in which he declared Monday, November 7, as American United Life Day in Indianapolis. And Indiana Insurance Commissioner H. P. "Pete" Hudson expressed congratulations and best wishes on behalf of his department and Indiana Governor Otis R. Bowen, who was unable to attend.

As part of the special festivities, Ruth Saylor, general files clerk, was presented the Elder Statesman Award, emblematic of her position as the home office employee with the longest record of continuous service to AUL. Ruth, who had been with the company for more than forty-two years, succeeded J. Harold Thompson, who retired September 30.

Chairman Reich and President Barlet also presented Elder Statesman

A huge cake in the shape of the AUL building was served at the reception following the company's one hundredth anniversary gala at Clowes Hall at Butler University on November 7, 1977.

This special medallion was designed for the company's hundredth anniversary celebration in 1977. It bears logos from United Mutual and American Central as well as an image of the AUL building.

Awards to two agents, Ted R. Bailey, of Dayton, Ohio, and John B. Tate, Sr., of Tulsa, Oklahoma, who had been with the company for more than half of its first century. Ted Bailey actually had the most years of service, going back to 1920 when he was hired as an accounting clerk in the home office, but John Tate, who was not able to attend the program, had the most years on the field force. He became an agent for American Central in 1923.

The finale of the hundredth anniversary celebration was a mammoth birthday cake and punch reception on the Clowes Hall stage that followed performances by the Purdue Glee Club, the Belles of Indiana, and an ensemble of dancers and instrumental and vocal musicians from Butler University. Master of ceremonies for the evening was David Letterman, recognized today as the popular host of *The Late Show* on CBS television. At the time of the centennial celebration, Letterman, a former Indianapolis radio and television personality, was a TV comedy writer and performer in Hollywood.

The Butler ensemble had been formed specifically to perform at the Indiana Society of Chicago dinner on December 3 at Chicago's Conrad Hilton Hotel. At that event, AUL was honored as the Hoosier Company of the Year, and Butler University was recognized as the Hoosier Educational Institution of the Year.

In the December issue of the *AULnews*, Reich summed up a very significant year this way:

> In 1977, we took great strides toward improving our group operation. We installed a new EDP system for credit insurance, a new EDP system for check writing, and a new EDP system for mortgage loan accounting. We have elected a woman to the AUL board of directors, installed an ultra-modern telephone system in the home office, modernized our word processing center, put in an attractive new cafeteria, and done many less noticeable but equally significant things to improve working conditions and to stay competitive in the marketplace.

When all the financial figures for the year were tabulated, they showed that AUL's assets had increased 17.3 percent for the year, increasing from $798 million to almost $936 million. The net gain from operations was $8.8 million, a 49.7 percent increase over the best previous year, which was 1976. And the face amount of life insurance sold was $1.7 billion, a one-year increase of 26.7 percent that reflects the first billion-dollar performance by the reinsurance division.

When *Fortune* magazine came out in the summer of 1978, American United Life Insurance Company—on the basis of those 1977 asset figures—ranked forty-seventh on the list of the Fifty Largest Life Insurance Companies in the United States.

Attractive by day, the AUL building was even more striking at night after outside lights were added.

In recognition of the nation's Bicentennial celebration in 1976 and to enhance the attractiveness of the AUL grounds, five flagpoles were erected in front of the home office. Displayed on the poles then were the American flag, plus flags for Indiana, Indianapolis, AUL, and the Bicentennial. In later years, the fifth flag was usually the state flag of a visitor to the company's home office.

CHAPTER 7

TALK OF A MOVE DOWNTOWN

It was April 18, 1977. All the product divisions seemed to be doing well, and plans were underway for the company's big centennial celebration coming up in November. At a meeting of the AUL executive committee that day, a new topic was being discussed. Chairman Jack Reich told the committee that, at the rate the company was growing, it would be out of space by 1985. What should they do?

They could build another addition on the home office, but, after already building two additions, where could they put another? They could build on the parking lot across Twenty-sixth Street, but then what would they do with employee parking? They could build a new building somewhere else, but, to do that, they would need a buyer for the present facilities. Who would want this big, old building and all that parking space?

The minutes of that executive committee meeting don't show what decisions were made that day. Probably none were. But Reich apparently left that meeting convinced that the company should build a new building and, to make that possible, he needed to find a buyer for the home office. He may even have had an idea where to begin looking.

His friend and former State Chamber of Commerce associate, John Barnett, remembers a telephone call he received: "I was chairman of the Ivy Tech board at the time, and he [Reich] called me one day and said, 'When you're going home this evening, why don't you stop past so I can talk with you a minute.' And I said, 'All right.' So, I stopped by and went up to his office. And on the Fall Creek side [of the AUL building]—Do you remember where it had AMERICAN UNITED LIFE INSURANCE COMPANY up there in the stone on the side?—he had a picture on his desk of that and, in place of that [name], he had lettered in INDIANA VOCATIONAL TECHNICAL COLLEGE. And he said, 'How would you like to see that?' I said, 'Great, but I don't know what the hell we would use for money to do it.'

"That was the first I had ever heard about it. Then I found out that was part of the grand plan to get AUL downtown as sort of the anchor for renovation, but, before they could do that, they had to dispose of the building. . . . We talked about it in our Ivy Tech board meeting and said, 'Yes, it would be great if we could do it, but what would we use for money?' "

At a meeting of the AUL executive committee on October 3, 1977, Reich reported that Ivy Tech was a prospective buyer for the home office. Out of the discussion that followed came a decision to call a special meeting of the AUL board and to report the situation to the rest of the board members and to seek their approval to appoint a building committee and to move ahead with plans to sell the building and select a site for a new one. That meeting was held a week later, on October 10, and Reich got the support of the full board and authorization to appoint a building committee.

Harold Ingersoll, a member of AUL's board and executive committee at the time, said that after some discussion in that meeting, "Jack said, 'You know we're going to have to have a building committee and how shall we go about it?' [Board Member] Freda Lockhart said, 'Well, it ought to be the executive committee,' and everyone agreed with that. That was it. So that became the building committee. No one opposed it, and, apparently Jack thought it was a good idea."

Actually, the building committee wound up being composed of four of the five executive committee members—Reich, Ingersoll, Harry Ice, and Dr. Donald Wood. The fifth member, President Les Barlet, was apparently left off so that he could concentrate on the day-to-day operations of the company.

When asked what specific instructions the AUL board gave the building

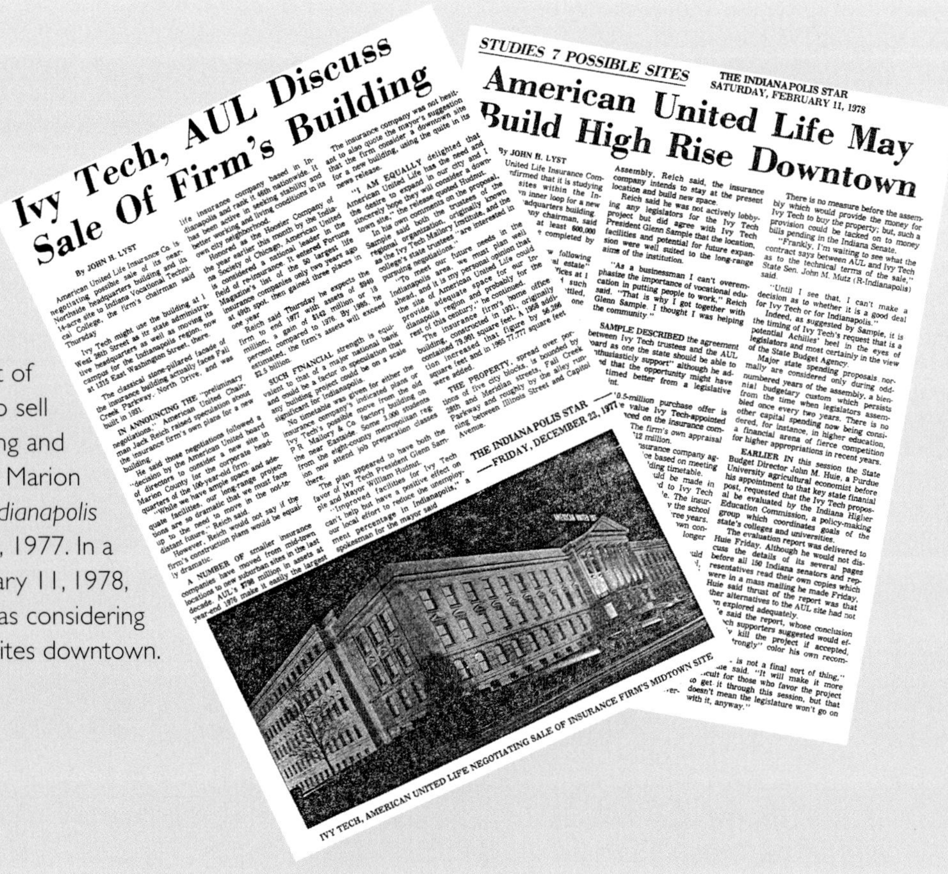
Ivy Tech, AUL Discuss Sale Of Firm's Building

STUDIES 7 POSSIBLE SITES
THE INDIANAPOLIS STAR SATURDAY, FEBRUARY 11, 1978
American United Life May Build High Rise Downtown

THE INDIANAPOLIS STAR —FRIDAY, DECEMBER 23, 1977

IVY TECH, AMERICAN UNITED LIFE NEGOTIATING SALE OF INSURANCE FIRM'S MIDTOWN SITE

The first announcement of "preliminary negotiations" to sell the Fall Creek building and relocate somewhere else in Marion County appeared in *The Indianapolis Star* on December 23, 1977. In a subsequent story on February 11, 1978, AUL confirmed that it was considering new building sites downtown.

committee, Ingersoll said, "Whatever Jack wanted to do." And obviously, Reich knew what he wanted to do. He began immediately to work with the Ivy Tech board and with state government leaders. Since Ivy Tech was a state college, the state was the place to go for funds to obtain a new Indianapolis campus for the college.

The public—and the employees of AUL—got their first glimpse of the future on Friday, December 23, when they saw the headline in *The Indianapolis Star* proclaiming IVY TECH, AUL DISCUSS SALE OF FIRM'S BUILDING. The accompanying story said in part:

> In announcing the "preliminary negotiations," American United Chairman Jack Reich raised speculation about the insurance firm's own plans for a new building. He said those negotiations followed a decision by the American United board of directors to consider a new site in Marion County for the corporate headquarters of the 100-year-old firm.

The Star story even noted that AUL, in its news release announcing the negotiations, opted to include a quote from Indianapolis Mayor William H. Hudnut III saying, "I am . . . delighted that American United Life has the need and the desire to expand in our city and I sincerely hope they will consider a downtown site."

In January 1978 the *AULnews* carried a story aimed at reassuring employees "that the home office will remain in Indianapolis and it will be several years before a move can take place." That story also used the mayor's comment about considering a downtown site.

A record snowfall of more than twenty inches closed down much of Indianapolis, including the AUL building, on January 26, 1978. The snow also created some wonderful opportunities for photographers.

By this time, the Indiana General Assembly was in session, the Ivy Tech purchase was getting some support, as well as some opposition, and AUL's selling price was being rumored as "probably less than $10 million" but possibly as high as $12 million for the AUL home office and fourteen acres of land. But this was a year the legislature had its "short" session. Major state spending proposals were normally considered only during odd-numbered years. The situation called for a strong selling job, and Reich, Mayor Hudnut, and Ivy Tech President Glenn Sample gave it all they had.

In an *Indianapolis Star* story on February 11, Reich confirmed that AUL was considering seven possible sites downtown, but he was also quoted as saying, if the project was not approved by the current session of the legislature, AUL would stay where it is and build new space. And it looked for a time as if that is what AUL would have to do. The Indiana Higher Education Commission said Ivy Tech needed to explore other possible sites, and a group of citizens began a campaign to get Ivy Tech to relocate to the Meadows area on East Thirty-eighth Street.

On March 5 the state legislature adjourned after approving a state budget that included $8.5 million that could be used by Ivy Tech or by the state to buy the AUL building or use the money for several other purposes. At that point, however, AUL and Ivy Tech had apparently agreed on a purchase price of $10.5 million.

On June 9 the Higher Education Commission, after lengthy debate, voted to recommend that Ivy Tech be allowed to buy the AUL home office, but it said the college should look elsewhere for a new home if it could not erase the $2 million gap on the price. Governor Otis Bowen took essentially the same position and, a few days later, the State Budget Committee, by a 2–2 vote, failed to recommend even that action. So, on June 20, Reich announced that AUL's board had voted to terminate negotiations. In a statement that touched all the chords, Reich said:

> We are a mutual company, owned by our policyholders, and our first obligation is to look out for their interests. For that reason, the company's board of directors voted today to terminate negotiations with Indiana Vocational Technical College. We have gone well beyond the time we said we would wait for Ivy Tech to obtain the necessary state approval to buy our building, and with construction costs continuing to go up, the board felt it could no longer tolerate the delays.
>
> As a company and as individuals, we are concerned about the unemployment that exists in Indianapolis despite great demand for skilled and semiskilled help. Unemployment in the Evansville and Fort Wayne areas is lower than in the Indianapolis metropolitan area. Ivy Tech, which has excellent facilities in those other cities, could be the difference, and partly in our own interest, we would like to see

> vocational education in Indianapolis expanded. But not at the expense of our policyholders.
>
> We are deeply appreciative of the active interest Mayor Hudnut took in trying to work out the purchase by Ivy Tech. We share his view that the sale of our building to Ivy Tech and our subsequent move to new facilities downtown would have been good for the entire community. What we thought was something in the public interest, however, has become a partisan issue. [Two Democrats on the State Budget Committee had voted against approving the sale.]

Reich concluded his statement by saying that, "in light of the delays and the unlikely prospect that a satisfactory agreement could be worked out," AUL was resuming plans to expand on its present site.

A few days later, Reich denied rumors that negotiation between AUL and Ivy Tech were still going on behind the scenes, but on July 17 Ivy Tech President Glenn Sample announced that Ivy Tech would "very likely" acquire the AUL property. The Ivy Tech president said, "Thanks to a generous pledge by the Lilly Endowment (revealed later to be $500,000), it appears that we are able to solve the financial problems that have plagued the negotiations." Reich said he had presented to his board of directors an offer of $9 million and that "President Sample and I will proceed immediately to prepare the necessary understanding which must be approved by the board, by the Ivy Tech regional and state boards and by the necessary state officials before we can finalize these negotiations."

There was still opposition, but on August 16 the State Budget Committee approved the deal on a 3–2 vote. On September 15, the State Finance Board

Harold G. Ingersoll, Jr., of New Castle, Indiana, served on AUL's board of directors from 1968 to 1995. Ingersoll was a member of the board's executive committee, as well as its building and salary and nominating committees, and he played a key role in planning for the new building. He was also president of Ingersoll Steel Division of Borg-Warner Corporation in New Castle for more than twenty years.

approved (Governor Otis Bowen and State Treasurer Jack New voted yes. State Auditor Mary Aikens Curry abstained.) And on October 19, Mayor Hudnut announced that the U.S. Environmental Protection Agency had advised him it had no requirements that would affect AUL's plans to build downtown despite questions that had been raised about the possible effect on the city's air quality.

The actual purchase price was $9.4 million—$8.5 million from the state, $500,000 from Lilly Endowment, and $400,000 in investment income from Ivy Tech. In addition, AUL was expected to pick up another $2.1 million by investing the money during the four years it would occupy its old facilities while its new building was being built. And AUL was allowed to call off the deal if it was not able to find a downtown site within six months.

On December 11—almost a year after going public with its plans—AUL announced that the Chicago office of the architectural firm of Skidmore, Owings and Merrill had been hired to design its new building and that Indianapolis-based Huber, Hunt and Nichols would be the construction manager. Reich said no site would be selected until the architects had time to evaluate the relative merits of several sites.

Nathaniel Owings, one of the founders of the architectural firm chosen to design the new AUL building was a native of Indianapolis and a graduate of Arsenal Technical High School. He was also a graduate of Cornell University, with honorary degrees from Butler, Ball State, and Indiana University. He founded his company in 1933 and in 1939 designed a traveling exhibit for AUL. That exhibit, dubbed the Pro-Motor, was used to publicize the American United Life Insurance Company name throughout the Midwest.

The Skidmore, Owings and Merrill firm was probably best known for designing the United States Air Force Academy, the Chase Manhattan Bank in New York, the Bank of America world headquarters in San Francisco, and the John Hancock Center and Sears Tower in Chicago.

Huber, Hunt and Nichols, construction manager for AUL, was founded in Indianapolis in 1942. It had built many of the city's largest buildings, including the City-County Building, the Federal Building, Market Square Arena, and Eli Lilly's research facilities. It was known nationally for work on the New Orleans Superdome and Riverfront Stadium in Cincinnati.

When Harold Ingersoll was asked how the decision was made to locate downtown, he said, "That was strictly Jack. Jack was very interested in the downtown, what would happen to the downtown with everyone moving to the outskirts, and he thought that it was very important that the building should support the downtown area. That was definitely his idea and, of course, everyone agreed with him on that."

Regarding what type of building to erect, Ingersoll recalled this incident: "Jack had the building committee members and their wives to a party at Meridian Hills Country Club. We were having cocktails before dinner, and Jack said, 'Now, what kind of a building do we want? Do we want a high-rise, or do we want a low-rise that would cover a whole block?' We had had the architects down prior to that, and the lead architect was most interested in having a low-rise building that would cover the whole AUL block. . . . Anyway, Jack said, 'How do you fellows feel about it?' There was an ashtray and a bud vase on the table, and Jack turned over the ashtray to represent the low-rise and the bud vase to represent the high-rise. And all of us, including Mrs. Reich, pointed to the bud vase. It was just that simple."

Ingersoll said he does not believe AUL set out to build the tallest building in the state. "We wanted a high-rise," he said. "To me, it never came up that it would be a floor or two higher than INB [Indiana National Bank]. Subconsciously, it may have been there, but it never came up."

As soon as it had a buyer for its building, AUL began working with the city to select a downtown site and acquire the property. On January 17, 1979, Mayor Hudnut asked the Metropolitan Development Commission to investigate the first block of Indiana Avenue, an area bounded by New York Street on the north, Capitol Avenue on the west, Ohio Street on the south, and

The downtown site as it looked when AUL acquired it in the summer of 1979. The AUL building was to occupy the block split by Indiana Avenue. The employee parking lot would fill the block to the north.

The Fox Theater, the last of almost twenty theaters that once dotted Illinois Street, was torn down in 1979 to make way for the new AUL Tower—but only after a brief effort by historic preservationists to save it. The Fox opened in 1909 and, while it was already closed when AUL bought the property, it was best remembered as the city's last burlesque house. After the demolition, AUL gave away bricks from the theater as souvenirs.

Illinois Street on the east. AUL said it was still considering three downtown locations, and the mayor said the investigation was "to gather data to ascertain whether assistance in land acquisition would be possible if assistance becomes necessary."

But that proved to be the building site. And city officials, who had already been quietly working with the AUL building committee for several months, acquired all the property AUL needed, doing it without resorting to condemnation. Archie Kuoppala, who had recently retired after nineteen years as administrator of the city's Division of Urban Renewal, came out of retirement to negotiate with the property owners of the Indiana Avenue block and the block to the north, which AUL wanted for employee parking. Again, it was a slow process, but on June 25 the city's Urban Renewal Division announced that it had completed negotiations for the purchase of the two downtown blocks.

On June 27 the Metropolitan Development Commission approved a $6,775,000 bid from AUL for the two-square block area, which had been designated as an urban renewal project. City officials said AUL's bid was $44,700 over the total amount of acquisition costs for the twenty-five parcels of land involved. That same day, Jack Reich announced that construction of AUL's new headquarters building would begin before the end of the year. He said the new building would be thirty to thirty-five stories high and contain 400,000 to 600,000 square feet of office space. At a news conference on July 2, Reich, Ivy Tech President Glenn Sample, and Mayor Hudnut announced completion of the complicated project that gave Ivy Tech a new headquarters at Twenty-sixth and Meridian and AUL a building site on the northwest side of the downtown. AUL's agreement with Ivy Tech was finally signed on September 12.

Demolition on the south block began in early September, and October 15 Reich announced that the AUL board of directors had approved construction of a thirty-eight-story office tower with three levels of underground parking. He said the company would use the fast-track method of construction, with excavating and foundation work being done while final design and engineering work is being completed, in order to have the building ready for occupancy by October 1, 1982. The building was to be 533 feet tall—the tallest building in Indiana by twenty-nine feet. At AUL's request, the block on which it would be located was designated as American Square.

Right in the middle of all of the excitement about the new building, the AUL family was shocked and saddened by the sudden death of President Les Barlet, who died at home on October 17 at the age of sixty-four. He had joined AUL in 1941 and had been promoted to president in 1977. He was active in the community and very popular with the work force at AUL. He would be missed.

On the very brisk morning of December 5, 1979, the ceremonial groundbreaking for the new building was held before more than one thousand spectators, including Governor Otis Bowen, Mayor William Hudnut, Ivy Tech President Glenn Sample, the AUL board members, and about five hundred home office employees, who were bused downtown for the occasion. Jack Reich presided and the first shovels of dirt were turned by four representatives of the field force and four representatives of the home office.

Representing the field force were General Agent James Comstock, CLU; Career Agent Francis "F" Quinn; Curly Thomas, vice president of group sales, and James Call, senior reinsurance account representative. The home office was represented by Cheryl Gentry, president of the AUL Employees Association; Cathie Morgan, president of the AUL Women's Club; Lillian Murphy, president of the AUL Twenty-Year Club, and Jim Long, president of the AUL Men's Club.

The groundbreaking took place almost exactly two years after AUL had revealed its negotiations with Ivy Tech. Now there would be a thirty-four-month wait for the new AUL Tower at One American Square to be ready for occupancy.

A caravan of buses brought more than 500 AUL employees downtown for the groundbreaking ceremonies.

The NEWS Photo, Patty Espich

AUL employes attend groundbreaking ceremonies today at new downtown headquarters site.

Downtown AUL Tower 'Starts'

By GERRY LaFOLLETTE

Groundbreaking ceremonies were today for the latest addition to downtown Indianapolis, the 37-story headquarters for American United Life Insurance Co.

Turning the first shovels of dirt on the northeast corner of Ohio Street and Capitol Avenue were four representatives of the insurance company's home office and four from the field force of the 100-year-old company, now in the top 50 life insurance companies in the country.

From the home office were presidents of four employe associations:

Cheryl Gentry
Cathie Morgan
Lillian Murphy
Jim Long.

From the field force were

Jim Comstock, Indianapolis
Francis "F" Quinn, Indianapolis
Curly Thomas, vice president of groups sales
Jim Call, reinsurance sales.

Also helping to mark the occasion were:

Jack Reich, AUL chairman
Bruce Graham, design partner of Skidmore Owings & Merrill, project architects
Robert Hunt, chairman of Huber Hunt & Nichols, construction manager
Gov. Otis Bowen
Mayor William Hudnut.

Also present were representatives of Top Notch, an organization of building trade unions and contractors.

Reich said, "We are at the midpoint; three years are behind us and three years are ahead of us."

More than 500 employes came to the groundbreaking in 10 chartered buses.

It was three years ago that the company considered expanding its present office at Meridian and Fall Creek by closing off 30th Street. Since then, with the help of state and local officials and the Legislature, that changed. Ivy Tech bought the headquarters and will move in after AUL moves out.

Hunt said, "excavation will start right after the first of the year. Foundation work will begin in the spring.

Continued on Page 13

The NEWS Photo, Joe Young

Model of 37-story AUL facility.

THE NEWS
Blue Streak
110th YEAR © 1979 The Indianapolis News 20 CENTS
INDIANAPOLIS, INDIANA, WEDNESDAY, DECEMBER 5, 1979

Kennedy Urges 'Shah' Debate

By PETER BROWN

WASHINGTON (UPI) — Sen. Edward Kennedy said today there ought to be public debate over whether the shah of Iran should be granted permanent asylum in the United States, and that such a debate might benefit the hostages held in Tehran.

Kennedy told a news conference he has no regrets about speaking out about the shah and said he does not think his critical comments endanger the hostages.

"We were told to be silent on Vietnam because they said such a debate wouldn't be healthy," Kennedy said. "I was asked a specific question and I gave what I thought was a responsible answer."

U.S. Shuts Embassy In Libya

WASHINGTON (AP) — The U.S. is closing its embassy in Libya until Col. Moammar Khadafy's government accepts responsibility for a mob that ransacked it last Sunday, the State Department said today.

With the announcement came a warning that relations will be cut if Libya rejects U.S. demands. "We do expect a satisfactory answer

The groundbreaking ceremonies were front-page news in the late edition of *The Indianapolis News* on December 5, 1979.

Chairman Jack Reich presided at the groundbreaking ceremonies. Special guests were seated in the stands behind him.

Indiana Governor Otis Bowen (left) and Indianapolis Mayor William Hudnut shared a shovel at the groundbreaking ceremonies.

Before construction workers could go up, they had to go down, as AUL wanted three levels of parking under its new building. This is the way the site looked March 20, 1980.

In April 1980 construction workers were pouring concrete for the building's foundation.

By February 1981 the distinctive, six-sided tower was beginning to take shape.

Even before the exterior work was complete, the AUL Tower had changed the look of downtown Indianapolis.

CHAPTER 8

DEFINITELY NOT A DULL YEAR — OR TWO

The ongoing story of AUL's efforts to get a buyer for its building and a suitable downtown location for its new office tower attracted most of the public attention during 1978 and 1979, but the work of building an insurance company continued as well.

In 1978 the face value of new life insurance sales was a company record $1.999 billion, up 15.3 percent over the previous year, and total income topped $300 million for the first time, also up more than 15 percent over 1977.

Personnel benefits for agents and employees were improved in 1978 and benefits for agents improved again in 1979. Also, the policy regarding retirement was changed to allow employees to work past age sixty-five if they chose.

In the first quarter of 1979, the company reached $10 billion of life insurance in force, double the amount it had just nine years earlier. The company reached $11 billion of insurance in force a few months later, and Chairman Jack Reich told employees, "In another ten years, we'll be selling that much in a single year."

In 1979, also, the reinsurance division celebrated its seventy-fifth anniversary. The individual division released a new generation of term policies and a new low-premium, whole life policy called Alpha 100, and work began on a program to link computer terminals in agency offices directly with the AUL computer in the home office. DART (Direct Access Remote Terminal), as the system was known, became operational in 1980.

While the new building was under construction, AUL treated Indianapolis to a free laser light show for three nights in July 1980, as it considered the idea of putting laser lights on top of the building as a form of identification. It turned out the laser beams could be seen only a few miles from the site, so the company gave up the idea. It later decided that the large American flag that now flies from an 80-foot pole atop the 533-foot building would identify the new city landmark.

One of the most significant events of 1980 occurred in May when the

AUL board of directors elected Jerry D. Semler as its new company president and board member, replacing Les Barlet, who had died the previous October.

Semler, one of AUL's top general agents at the time, was the first president in the company's history to come from a background in insurance sales. A 1958 graduate of Purdue University, he joined AUL in 1959 after six months of military service. He began working in the policy issue department, but five months later he became an agent, working in AUL's Indianapolis agency for General Agent James Comstock. In 1960, he married Rosemary Reich, a daughter of Jack and Jean Reich. In December 1971 he opened his own agency in Indianapolis, continuing to sell for AUL.

Semler became a Chartered Life Underwriter (CLU) in 1976, the same year he became a life member of the industry's Million Dollar Round Table. He assumed the presidency of AUL on August 1, 1980. Reich remained as AUL's chairman and chief executive officer. (See story on Semler on pages 102–105.)

The selection of Semler as company president stirred conversation at AUL for a short time, since few people in the company knew he was being considered for the job. The field force was particularly pleased to see one of its own get the job. But most eyes remained focused on the new building.

By late summer of 1980, the new building was beginning to rise from the ground, and at the old home office a company-wide housecleaning campaign was underway. It was the first of several such events to be conducted over the next two years to get employees to clean out cabinets, desks and bookcases and

Jerry D. Semler was elected president and a member of the AUL board of directors in May 1980, replacing F. Leslie Barlet, who died October 17, 1979.

to throw away unneeded files, correspondence, and accumulated "junk." The purpose, of course, was to reduce the amount of material that would have to be moved—and stored—in the new building.

Ken McGlothlin, vice president for policy contract services, chaired the Record Destruction Committee, which was in charge of the clean-up. To add a little fun and get the job done, Policy Title Specialist Mary Babbitt, a well-known and well-liked employee, was given the added title of "taskmaster" and assigned to go around to all the departments to see that the work was accomplished. The first week of this "Toss It" clean-up campaign resulted in almost twelve tons of trash being thrown away. Unusual finds during the cleaning process were a film made in 1960 of the installation of the NCR 304 computer, a 1955 taped speech by Clarence Jackson, and a mortgage loan agreement for twenty-five dollars marked PAID on March 11, 1909.

By the time this first week of housecleaning began, Dr. John Pearson, vice president for medical and underwriting, was already hard at work planning the move downtown. Aware that Dr. Pearson was about to retire, Chairman Reich had prevailed on him to take on the job of moving coordinator. He was now up to his elbows in floor plans, office equipment inventories, and reams of paper documenting everything one needs to know to move an insurance company.

At about this same time, some 85,000 cubic feet of Indiana limestone was being cut out of the rolling hills near Bedford, Indiana, by the Indiana

After a decade of growth in the 1970s and with the new building going up, AUL reported its progress in a full-page ad that appeared in *The Indianapolis Star* and *The Wall Street Journal* on April 25, 1980.

Limestone Company. These blocks of limestone would soon be cut, shaped and textured to provide the exterior skin of the new AUL building.

Later that year, it was announced that Morrison's Management Services would operate the cafeteria in the new building. Morrison's had a chain of cafeterias, mostly in the South. This cafeteria would seat six hundred and serve AUL employees, other tenants of the building, and the general public.

It was also revealed that Johnson Controls, Inc., was designing a computerized building management system that would make One American Square one of the safest high-rise buildings in the nation. One system would handle fire management, environmental controls, and building security.

To detect fire, the system would have sensors throughout all floor areas, as well as uninhabited areas, such as ventilation ducts. When the system detects smoke or a potential fire, it automatically calls the fire department and indicates where the fire is located in the building. The computer brings selected elevators to the ground floor where they are operated by firefighters using manual key controls. Prerecorded voice commands alert occupants on the floor where the alarms are set off, as well as those immediately above and below.

Stairwells are pressurized to keep smoke from entering them. The computer system activates fans and dampers to clear smoke from the floors and to prevent a fire from spreading throughout the building. The computer can also activate the sprinkler system. Firefighters can be directed from a special fire control panel on the ground floor, where the officer in command has control of elevators and important building equipment. A computer printer records all of the systems' activities during an emergency. The system also gives firefighters access to an emergency public address microphone, a two-way intercom system and outside phone lines.

For security, surveillance cameras cover all of the building's entrances, the employee parking lots north of the building, the three levels of underground parking, the loading dock, and the main lobby of the building. Cameras are also in selected elevators for after-hours sound-and-visual monitoring. An identification card system is used by employees in off-hours to activate the elevators, limiting access to only those floors where an employee is authorized to work. The system alerts security personnel through a central computer whenever an illegal card is used, when a guard does not check on a watch tour, or when the system is tampered with in any way. The computer also controls the building's heating and cooling, humidity and ventilation, and the building's lighting system.

The building management system, technically known as the JC/85, was one of the single largest capital outlays in the building, costing about $2 million. "The expense, however, is more than offset by the potential savings in human lives," Reich said in announcing the decision to purchase the Johnson Controls system.

Heating and cooling for the new building was accomplished by a unique well-water heat exchanger system that the architects claimed made the building one of the most energy-efficient high-rises in the country. The idea for such a system solved a major problem too. Under the building is an aquifer—in fact, it is under much of downtown Indianapolis. An aquifer is an underground layer of sand or gravel that contains water, and the building designers faced the problem of keeping ground water out of the three levels of underground parking and the deep basements. Instead of just pumping the water out, which would be an ongoing expense, they decided to use the water source for heating and cooling the building.

Underground water temperature remains fairly constant at 60 to 65 degrees year-round. That makes it warmer than outdoor winter temperatures and cooler than outdoor summer temperatures and an excellent source for heating and cooling. Four deep wells were dug to tap into the water source. As the designers worked on the system, more advantages became apparent. The heat exchanger eliminated the need for expensive cooling towers and piping, boilers, and stacks. It also does away with flue gas air pollution and requires less maintenance and smaller refrigeration units and uses a very dependable energy supply—water.

Later, it was discovered that by dumping the water in the nearby city canal after using it for warming or cooling the building, AUL was able to provide fresh, flowing water that kept the canal clean and attractive. To handle AUL's water, a 48-inch pipe had to be installed, running parallel to Ohio Street. Since the canal had to be drained to permit installation of the pipe, the White River Park Development Commission decided to take advantage of the project's timing and clean up the canal itself. The canal was drained from Seventeenth Street down to Military Park and private contractors began a huge clean-up project in which they removed 360 cubic yards of trash and debris.

At his annual meeting with all employees in April 1981, Chairman Reich reported that work on the new building was on schedule and the move would probably begin in August 1982. (It turned out to be September.) He also told employees a number of other things they had been asking about. Nearly all of the furniture in the new building would be new, he told them. AUL would occupy floors two through nine, and employees would have comfortable work areas and enough room to handle five years of growth. Everyone currently on the payroll would have a free parking space across the street from the building and, for those who chose to ride the bus, the company was considering providing bus passes at a discount. (It did and still does.) Everyone should continue to clean out old files since space used for storage could not be used by employees or rented to tenants.

On July 30, 1981, about 250 invited guests assembled for the traditional topping-out ceremony, where the last steel beam was raised into place. This particular steel beam, twelve feet long and painted white, contained signatures of AUL employees and agents. In addition, it carried a small tree, an American flag, and a bag of rather unusual items.

The use of the tree dates back hundreds of years to Europe where the evergreen was considered a good luck charm. The flag is an American tradition started by ironworkers. But M. William Lutholtz, AUL's publications editor, got interested in the subject, did some research and added some other topping-out items: a jar of chicken blood (the Chinese did this as a gesture of thanks to the gods), some eggs (the Scandinavians didn't want the gods to get hungry), some handcuffs to shackle any contemporary versions of the Persian water spirits, and some corn to feed the horse of Norse god Odin. Since Alfred J. Stokely, retired chairman of Stokely-Van Camp, was a member of the AUL board of directors, Lutholtz chose a can of Stokely-Van Camp's Finest Whole Kernel Golden Corn.

At the topping out, Indiana Lieutenant Governor John M. Mutz and Indianapolis Deputy Mayor David Frick made brief congratulatory speeches on behalf of the state and city, and Indiana National Bank Chairman Thomas Miller presented Reich with a crystal bison as he good naturedly conceded INB's position as owner of the tallest building in the state. The bison was the corporate symbol of the bank.

Not long after the building reached its full height, it was announced that the top floor of the building would be the home of the Skyline Club, a private dining club owned and managed by the Club Corporation of America. (Actually, the Skyline Club is on the thirty-sixth floor. Floors thirty-seven and thirty-eight, the top floors, are mechanical floors.)

As soon as the calendar flipped to 1982, AUL employees began counting down to moving day and the field force was given the first information on Celebration Indy '83, to be May 12–15, 1983, when they would have a chance to participate in the official grand opening of the building. It would be about six months after AUL got in the new building before landscaping would be done, the Skyline Club would be open, and upper floors would be finished.

The possible demise of Acapulco Joe's Mexican Restaurant was a much bigger public relations problem for AUL than the Fox Theater's destruction had been. Because it was on land that AUL had designated for a parking lot, the restaurant had remained open during AUL's construction, serving hundreds of satisfied customers every day. *Indianapolis News* columnist R. K. Shull wrote on April 19, 1982, "The city is about to trade off one of its most delightful living cultural treasures for twelve lousy parking spaces." Fortunately, the problem was finally solved when Joe's agreed to move to the other side of Illinois Street.

There was a bit of nostalgia as groups such as AUL's Twenty-Year Club began having their last parties in the old building, but there was no containing the excitement as department heads laid out new work areas on building floor plans, ordered new furniture and equipment, and made arrangements to pack and move everything that needed to go. On September 3, the fifth and final "Toss It" clean-up session was held. More than forty-eight tons of trash had been removed during the first four sessions, but apparently no one was counting this time because a final measurement of what was thrown away was never reported. And with all of this effort, it was estimated it would still require more than 16,000 boxes to pack up what was left.

The print shop was the first to move, on September 10, followed by the supply department on September 17. Those two departments moved at night to avoid interrupting the construction crews still working on the floors above. Crown Moving and Storage, the local agents for Wheaton Van Lines, handled the transportation. Print shop supervisor Bob Woods said, "It took them from 5:30 P.M. right up to the stroke of midnight to get us down there. We were all tired for a whole week after that but it all went fairly well." Mail and supply supervisor Roger Mills said, "We finished packing the last box at 5:05 and the movers showed up at 5:30. It took us three days to pack for the move." The actual move took until 6:05 the next morning. The supply department moved thirty-eight hundred boxes, completely filling five moving vans.

Before the topping-out ceremony on July 30, 1981, AUL employees, agents and local dignitaries—including Indianapolis Mayor William H. Hudnut III (right), with Chairman Jack Reich—signed the last beam to be put in place.

Everything went well until a water pipe burst in the late afternoon of September 22, flooding the lobby and the two lower levels where printing and supply were located. No one was injured and the building management staff quickly repaired the leak. Water was ankle-deep in the supply area for a while and several boxes of printed forms and supplies were damaged, but the departments recovered quickly.

The rest of the departments moved early in October on a systematic plan where members of a department left everything packed in boxes in their old office one evening and found those boxes sitting in their new office the next morning. The last employees arrived downtown on October 14, and what a day that was.

Mayor Hudnut proclaimed October 14, 1982, to be "American United Life Day." The celebration began at 5:30 that morning with a live radio broadcast from the thirty-sixth floor (the Skyline Club was not there yet) with WIBC radio personality Gary Todd interviewing Jack Reich and others. Then, as employees arrived at work between 7 and 8 o'clock, they got a big surprise. Members of the Butler University marching band and a large welcome banner greeted them as they approached the building from the parking lot.

At the New York Street entrance, the Merchants Bank costumed "frogs" and the National Sports Festival mascot, "Sneakers," danced to high-spirited tunes of the band and passed out balloons and clackers.

After a brief ceremony, workmen at the top of the thirty-eight-story structure anchored the last beam in place. The special beam carried an American flag, a small evergreen, and a bag of items from different traditions, all intended to bring the new building good luck.

In the lobby of the building, the employees were met by Mayor Hudnut and board members of the Commission for Downtown, who welcomed them and offered coffee, doughnuts and apples provided by the Indiana Restaurant Association. Throughout the day, television camera crews interviewed employees and photographed building highlights for their evening newscasts. At 4:30 P.M. the Commission for Downtown and the Merchants Association hosted a reception for AULers on Monument Circle. A buffet dinner, drinks, and the tunes of the Preservation Band kept the merriment going until early evening.

On October 27 in a ceremony on the front steps of the old home office, Reich handed over the keys to the building to Ivy Tech's board chairman, Wendell D. Vandivier, and Ivy Tech's acting president, John V. Barnett. Unfortunately, two men who played key roles in bringing this all about were not there to see the results of their efforts. Glenn Sample, the president of Ivy Tech who fought to get the right and the money to buy the AUL building, died of a heart attack not long after signing the purchase agreement, and Harry T. Ice died September 8, 1982, just days before AUL began moving into its new building. Ice was vice chairman of the AUL board of directors, a member of the building committee, and one of Jack Reich's closest friends and advisers.

Summarizing the events of 1982, Reich later told AUL employees, "It was definitely *not* a dull year." Neither was 1983.

By spring the building was ready to be shown off to the public. The Skyline Club opened April 8, and the first public event in the building, on

On October 27, 1982, Chairman Jack Reich (second from right) handed the keys to the old AUL building to Wendell D. Vandivier, Ivy Tech's board chairman. Attending the ceremony were John V. Barnett (left), acting president of Ivy Tech, and Edmund Genier, AUL's mortgage loan vice president, who had had primary responsibility for the building when AUL occupied it.

April 24, was a dinner-dance sponsored by the Women's Committee of the Indiana State Symphony Society. It was called "Symphony of Life," and a special part of the evening's entertainment was the premiere performance of a unique symphonic composition based on the AUL Tower and entitled "Building Music." It had been composed by Brad Garton of Columbus, Indiana, who said, "The basic sounds of construction of the AUL building that I heard daily, plus the unusual shape of the building, impelled me to write this music." It was played by the Indianapolis Symphony, which also played for dancing in the AUL lobby. About 450 people attended the sold-out event, some dining in Morrison's Cafeteria, some in the Skyline Club. Most took tours of the building led by specially trained AUL employees who volunteered their service.

Then came Celebration Indy '83, which began May 10 with meetings for the company's general agents, associate general agents, and group sales representatives. AUL agents arrived May 12 for three days of activities that included tours of the building, tours of Indianapolis attractions, sales meetings, award presentations, and a very rainy Saturday spent at the Indianapolis Motor Speedway. The first day of qualifications for the 500-Mile Race were washed out, but the guests got to see some late-afternoon practice, tour the garage area, and visit the Speedway Museum. A dinner-dance on Saturday night and a Sunday brunch at the Skyline Club closed out the special celebration.

The next few months saw AUL, the architects, and the builders receive several awards—for innovative design, for landscaping, for the well-water

Trees and shrubs were placed in the courtyard garden by August 26, 1982—moving day couldn't be far away!

heating and cooling system, and for flying the American flag on top of the building. Harold Ingersoll, a member of AUL's board and its building committee, said, "We wanted a quality building. We built it first-class all the way." That was now obvious to everyone. AUL earlier had said the building was going to cost about $50 million, but knowledgeable people later said the amount was likely closer to $80 million.

When AUL employees had a party October 13, 1983, to celebrate one year in their new building, sections of the old building were already being used by Ivy Tech for computer classes and other kinds of technical training. Some renovation work was still going on, however, and it would be awhile before the community could see and appreciate how well Ivy Tech fit in its new environment.

While AUL and Ivy Tech were working hard to close their deal on the Fall Creek property, many persons in the community were saying the school didn't need the AUL building, wouldn't make good use of it, and wouldn't maintain it as well as AUL had. In time, Indiana Vocational Technical College proved them wrong on every count. Downtown, American United Life Insurance Company grew and prospered as never before.

When the move began in September 1982, moving vans lined up at the old building each afternoon to pick up boxes packed that day by employees. Much of the moving was done at night to minimize the disruption of business and downtown traffic.

Mayor William Hudnut declared October 14, 1982, "American United Life Day." The move was complete and, as AUL employees arrived at work that day at the New York Street entrance, they were greeted by a band from Butler University, costumed mascots from the Indiana Sports Corporation and Merchants National Bank, and members of the Commission for Downtown.

Dr. John S. Pearson, AUL's recently retired vice president for medical and underwriting, catches his breath about midway through the move. Pearson spent the better part of two years planning and coordinating the company's relocation downtown.

Although the thirty-sixth floor, where the Skyline Club would be located in a few months, was not even fully enclosed on October 14, WIBC Radio's morning man Gary Todd (right) did his broadcast from there anyway. AUL Chairman Jack Reich was one of his on-air guests.

In the lobby, the employees were offered coffee, doughnuts, and apples provided by the Indiana Restaurant Association.

The BMS room is the nerve center of the building. BMS stands for "Building Management System," and it is from here that staff members keep tabs on building operations and security twenty-four hours a day, seven days a week.

Even before the new building was finished, AUL was running ads such as this one in locally delivered copies of several national magazines. The ads were designed by Lacy Advertising.

Any way you look at it.

The new American United Life building at One American Square is a dramatically unique building. Thirty-eight stories towering over downtown Indianapolis will offer spectacular views from all sides of the six-sided structure. Below the 38-story tower will lie 700 spaces in three levels of underground parking.

A striking three-story, glass-covered atrium lobby accentuated with a warm-toned granite floor and rich dark green marble walls will welcome all who enter the new American United Life Building at One American Square. An open garden courtyard will resemble a miniature tree-filled park, complete with a fountain and lagoon. Its beauty will reflect on the lobby's fine shops, the inviting Morrison-managed cafeteria, the auditorium and a banking center.

A highly sophisticated computerized building management system will be employed to provide the maximum in high-rise building security, fire detection and protection, life safety and environmental control. The building will have a sprinkler system throughout.

Convenient, Unique, Prestigious, Secure, Safe. . . . any way you look at it, the American United Life Building at One American Square is a great location for you.

For Leasing Information Call Robert Lauth at Klein & Kuhn 317-634-6666

A·U·L®

American United Life • Indianapolis

We have been guaranteeing futures for more than 100 years.

The new AUL Tower, with the American flag as a dramatic identifier, dominated the Indianapolis skyline in 1983. At the time it was the state's tallest structure—533 feet tall, twenty-nine feet taller than what was then the Indiana National Bank building. The flagpole on the roof adds another eighty feet.

Jerry D. Semler

(The following article was written by M. William Lutholtz in 1980 and appeared in the AULnews, of which he was editor, under the headline We know he's the President, but who *is* Jerry Semler, anyway?)

In college he was known as something of an entrepreneur. He had paid his way through Purdue, waiting tables in fraternity and sorority houses. He started his own tuxedo rental business on campus, and then diversified into flower sales by selling orchid corsages with the rented tuxes. With a growing circle of thirty agents working under him, he got into other ventures, selling fraternity jewelry, operating a Coke and candy concession, and a laundry business.

Eventually he got into the car business with a line of hearses that he purchased, planning to sell them at a profit to the Purdue fraternities as party wagons. He bought the hearses from a Chicago dealer and drove them down to West Lafayette, only to discover that the frat houses didn't have the money to buy them after all.

Undaunted, he started up a direct mail campaign, extolling the virtues of hearses used as party wagons. "I mailed out the brochures and found my prospects and sold the cars," he recalls. Who bought them? "American Legion posts," he says. "They thought it was a great idea!"

People say that early business experiences are often the most powerful influences on a career. If that is true, then the resourcefulness that Jerry Semler exhibited on the campus of Purdue University was certainly a good gauge of his future success as an insurance agent. It might have even been a harbinger of the day when he would be named president of American United Life.

Jerry Doran Semler was born in Indianapolis March 5, 1937, the son of Henry and Mary Semler. His father was an engineer, working as plant manager for a local manufacturing firm. His mother stayed home to raise the family—Jerry and, later, his two sisters, Nancy and Vicki.

Jerry was still quite young when America became involved in World War II, but he wasn't so young that he couldn't let the war years teach him his first lessons in business. Like thousands of other youngsters in those days, he was out going door-to-door selling plant seeds to neighbors for their "Victory Gardens." Discovering that plant seeds only had a seasonal demand, he was soon supplementing his income by selling Christmas cards and delivering *The Indianapolis Times*.

When Jerry was a young teenager, his father was named plant manager for General Electric and the family moved to Decatur, Illinois, where Jerry attended his first three years of high school. His father then took a position with Seiger Refrigeration and the family moved to Evansville, Indiana, where Jerry graduated from Bosse High School.

He had skipped eighth grade in order to get out of high school early. He thought at first that he would try to follow his father into engineering, so he enrolled at Purdue. "It didn't take me too long to figure out that engineering just wasn't my bag at all," he recalls. "What I liked was working with people, selling things, dealing with people on a one-to-one basis, so I switched to Industrial Economics—Purdue's business school." On the side, he was developing every potential campus business that he could get his hands on.

During spring break in 1957, Jerry went to Florida. One of his sister's sorority friends wanted him to meet a certain girl by the name of Rosemary Reich. They had been attending Purdue together—she was a year behind Jerry—but had somehow never managed to meet. Her father was something of a big wheel in business circles, being the executive vice president of the Indiana State Chamber of Commerce. But why should that stop Jerry? Wasn't he an entrepreneur in his own right?

After Florida, the two continued dating regularly, even after Jerry's graduation in 1958. That summer, the sight of Jerry's still-unsold hearses parked in the driveway at Jack Reich's house raised some occasional comments. One evening, the head of the Indianapolis Chamber of Commerce, Bill Book, and his wife, arrived late for dinner, apologizing to Reich for having been unaware of "the unfortunate death in the family." Asked what on earth he was talking about, Book pointed to the black hearse in the driveway. "Oh, that!" said Reich. "He's just dating my daughter!"

After announcing his engagement to Rosie, Jerry decided that he ought to start looking for a career with a bit more future than the campus concessions. "Ever since I was a kid, I had always been involved in some kind of partnership or sole proprietorship. I guess I was attracted to life insurance because it offered me a chance to be an entrepreneur, my own boss."

He came to Indianapolis and visited American United Life and several other local life insurance companies. "I told them what I had been doing and what I wanted to do. Several of them were ready to just put me out in the field to start selling."

At that time, however, military service was obligatory for unmarried men, so he fulfilled his military training requirement with a six-month stint in the army. "When I got out, Howard Alltop called me up and asked me to drop by AUL to talk. He said that he felt I would be better off if I worked a regular job in the home office for a few months and then went out into the field. This sounded good to me, and it gave me a chance to get my things moved down to Indianapolis from Purdue, so in March 1959, I started working in Policy Issue. Maryrose Rees helped train me in that department."

His real goal, however, was to become an agent, which he attained in August that year, working in "F" Quinn's unit at Jim Comstock's agency in Indianapolis. He was in on the ground floor of a business that he felt would provide him with "interesting work and a chance to grow." On February 27, 1960, Jerry and Rosie were married.

Looking back on his first years as an insurance agent, Jerry recalled, "One thing about insurance—it's not the easiest business to get established in, especially during the early years. It's a people business, a service business, that requires a lot of long hours and hard work."

Some of those working hours were spent with Curly Thomas, who was then regional group manager for AUL. Curly went out on the road with Jerry to show him the ropes of group sales.

"I remember the first call we went out on together was a company up in Noblesville. We did a lot of work on the case, studying and getting up a presentation. We went up and made our pitch and the guy told us that he was taking the business to another company," says Curly. "On the way back, Jerry was really furious, wasting all that time on somebody who'd already made up his mind to go with somebody else. I told him things would get better. Sure enough, after that we wrote up the Indiana Motor Truck Association. We traveled all over the state on that one, from South Bend to Evansville. We worked hard to get it, but the IMTA has grown into one of the largest group accounts on the book.

"Then things started popping and we got the Indiana Lumber Builders' Supply Association and a lot of others," Curly recalls. "I hate to think how many hours and miles we logged in to get those accounts, but it was profitable to the company and profitable for both of us. Along the way, Jerry became a very able student of group sales. And later he oriented all the people in his agency toward group products. He was the most successful group agent that I worked with at AUL in all the time that I was there."

Jerry was named a unit manager in January 1965. He was becoming more confident with his work and building a solid clientele and wanted to expose more people to the career opportunities of the insurance industry.

Two years later, he was treated to the unusual coincidence of seeing his father-in-law named board chairman and chief executive officer of AUL. Jack Reich had been serving on the AUL board for ten years but left his full-time position as chairman of the Indianapolis Water Company to fill the vacancy created by the retirement of AUL Chairman Clarence Jackson.

In December 1971, Jerry decided to take the next major step in his career—opening his own agency. "It wasn't something that I just jumped into. I had been in management since 1965. Even once the opportunity to start an agency became available, I waited about a year

Jerry Semler, 1980.

before I decided to make the move," he says.

He started the Semler Agency with agents Wayne McHargue, CLU, and Harvey Rau. That first year, they brought in $80,000 in premium, ranking seventeenth in the company. McHargue says that the overriding philosophy of the agency was to do business in a "family" atmosphere. "We decided at the beginning that life's too short to build an agency with all kinds of production squabbles and one guy trying to be a superstar at everybody else's expense. We decided that it was better to build the agency through cooperation and sharing. Whenever we brought in a new person for the agency, we tried to use the criterion: 'How well will this person fit into our agency family?' If someone didn't fit into that philosophy, even if they were highly productive, we'd encourage them to go somewhere else."

That "family" philosophy apparently paid off. The agency should finish this year with $400,000-plus production, one of the top five agencies with AUL. The "family" has grown from a three-agent operation to an eleven-agent firm. In that time, only three agents have left the agency. "We hope that the success of our agency philosophy is reflected in the agency's low turnover rate," says McHargue.

Jerry qualified for AUL's Leaders Club in 1960 and again in 1962. In 1963, he made the list for President's Club and has attended every President's Club since them. In 1978, based on his performance and the performance of his agency, he attended both clubs.

In 1976 he completed all the requirements for designation as a Chartered Life Underwriter. That same year, he qualified to become a life member of the Million Dollar Round Table.

If the "family" philosophy did well for Jerry in his agency, it worked equally well at home. Jerry and Rosie are now parents of seven children, three boys and four girls, who range from age nineteen to ten.

He has also managed to stay involved in community activities. He served for fifteen years as president of the house board of his fraternity, Alpha Tau Omega, and is still active with them as treasurer. He is a director of the 500 Festival Associates, and in 1980 served as chairman of the 500 Festival Parade. A member of the Indianapolis Chamber of Commerce, he serves on the Citizen's Speedway Committee.

Jerry is a director of the Indiana Sports Corporation, a nonprofit group dedicated to furthering amateur athletics in Indiana. He is a past president of the Museum of Indian Heritage. He has served as chairman of the Metropolitan Division of United Way. He has also been very active in local Boy Scout activities.

"Somehow he manages to divide his time between home and the office, and he does things with each of the children," says Rosie. "The agency demanded a lot of his time, and the presidency will probably require even more time, but I think Jerry's proven that you can be a good father and a successful businessman at the same time."

So how did the family find out about the fact that Dad was getting a new job? "I remember it very clearly," Rosie says. "Jerry told me that he had to go down and talk to what he thought was the Building Committee about something. He figured that they were going to ask him to move his agency into the new home office building.

"He'd just signed a new lease on his office in Castleton and told me that he was hoping they wouldn't try to talk him into giving up that lease. The first day he was supposed to meet with them, he couldn't make it. They set up another meeting later, and he walked out the door saying he hoped he wouldn't need to have his lease with him."

Jerry came home that evening with news to tell his wife. "But he wanted to wait until he'd have a chance to tell me alone," says Rosie. "After all the kids were settled, he told me that the Executive Committee had called him down there to tell him that he was being considered along with several others for the presidency of the company."

"I was sure they wanted to talk to me about leasing space," says Jerry. "I had no idea that they were considering me to become president of the company. I had an awful lot of sleepless nights making the decision. I spent a lot of time thinking about it.

"A lot of what made me decide to accept it was the challenge of being able to help more people. I mean, that's one of the things that got me into the insurance business in the first place—the chance to be in a business that is set up in order to help people and help the community.

"Some people think that the only reason an agent leaves the field is because he doesn't like to sell. That's wrong, dead wrong. I loved selling, and I loved working with people in the field. I still do," he says. "But there are other challenges, other kinds of opportunities that this job offers.

"I suppose a lot of people are waiting to see what I'm like, what kind of president I'm going to be. Some of the agents in the field probably think I've 'jumped ship.' And probably some of the people in the home office figure I'm going to give everything to the agents.

"I hope I'm going to be able to help people see that we are all really one company, that we are all part of AUL together, even though we all wear different hats and we all have different roles to play," he says.

"Right now, I've been spending most of my time trying to learn as much as I can about the internal functions of the company, trying to get to know as many people as I can. Of course, many of the home office people already know me, know who I am and how I operate.

"I've spent half my life working for AUL. It's been my only job since college. I'm not an outsider. I think the most important thing I have to offer this company is the experience in insurance that I've had as an agent and a general agent. I think that should be a good contribution to the future of the company."

It is interesting to note that Jerry Semler is the first president in the 102-year history of AUL to come to that position from a background in insurance sales. He notes that this seems to be a more common occurrence in the industry nationwide. "I'm at least the third field person this year who's been named president of a major insurance company. It may just be that more companies are realizing that they need more input from field-experienced people in the top management of their companies. That's what I am, and that's where I come from."

Galen Meyers with the Brungardt-Gregg agency in Topeka, Kansas, is one of AUL's top-performing agents. He's also one of Jerry Semler's oldest friends and business associates. The two of them started out with AUL the same year, and through meetings and conventions they formed a lasting friendship.

"I feel very good about seeing Jerry in that seat. He can relate to being an agent, since he was one. And I think he can relate to the home office people since he's always worked with them closely," says Galen. "His whole life has been AUL. It's his home and his whole fulfillment."

Galen says that he tried to measure Jerry against his immediate predecessor, President Les Barlet. "What I admired in Les Barlet was his tremendous individual qualities. He had a listening ear for everyone. He could relate to problems and then look for ways to solve them. Jerry has a lot of those same kinds of qualities about him.

"The thing about Les, the thing that really made him great, was that he never went around reminding you that he was 'The President' of AUL. He didn't have to because people respected him naturally. Jerry's a lot like that. Given the opportunity, I think he's going to serve this company very well. He's the president, and I think the best any of us can do is to support him and help make this company grow."

A Friend in the City-County Building

AUL's DECISION TO locate a new headquarters building in downtown Indianapolis, instead of a suburban location, represented a crucial turning point in the city's history. It created, as it were, a tipping point. It set a trend. It started the dominos tipping. "If AUL is coming downtown, we can too." Other businesses decided to stay in, or relocate to, downtown. New construction cranes began to dot the city skyline. Momentum for downtown revitalization gathered a good head of steam. And the rest, as they say, is history. But it all started in the board room of AUL.

Chairman Jack Reich, the building committee (Reich, Dr. Don Wood, Harry Ice, and Harold Ingersoll), and the entire board, recognized that the centrifugal forces of suburbanization were pulling vitality from downtown. When the company decided to move from Fall Creek and Meridian to new headquarters, they had two choices: a suburban location nearer to the geographical center of their work base; or downtown. Persuaded by their commitment to a strong Indianapolis center city and agreeing with our city's policy of trying to encourage urban reinvestment without discouraging suburban investment, the board decided on downtown.

When I was contacted about their possible relocation in mid-1978, I set in play a series of meetings with their building committee. Over the course of seventeen months, Deputy Mayor Dave Frick and I "negotiated" with the AUL team in countless meetings at their Fall Creek address. We showed them five different sites downtown, and ultimately, the Indiana Avenue site was decided upon. The city made several commitments to make this site attractive. We relocated a sewer line, vacated a portion of Indiana Avenue, assembled twenty-five small pieces of property (without using eminent domain), assisted in relocating several businesses, and provided AUL with ten years of tax abatement. We also worked with Lilly Endowment to find a new use—Ivy Tech—for the Fall Creek property. A ground breaking on Indiana Avenue was held on December 5, 1979, and the new building, the tallest skyscraper at the time in the state, was opened for business on October 14, 1982.

Many times in the years since, I have referred to this decision as an example of enlightened corporate citizenship at its best. I will always believe that civic pride, a deeply held belief in our city's future, and a realization that "you can't be a suburb of nothing," played a key role in shaping AUL's determination that it would be in the best interest of the company and the city to locate downtown. The construction of this beautiful building and the people and business it brought to downtown Indianapolis changed the psychology of our community and truly started the city on its path of downtown revitalization.

Thank you, AUL!

Bill Hudnut
Mayor (1976–1991)

Indianapolis Mayor William H. Hudnut III addressed AUL employees at a party on Monument Circle to welcome the company and its people to the downtown business district.

CHAPTER 9

A Tower of Strength

The new AUL Tower—the tallest building in the state at the time—attracted lots of attention, giving the company more visibility in the community than ever before. When people wanted a peek inside or a chance to view the city from the upper floors, AUL had a group of employees trained and available to give guided tours.

When people wanted to run up the 37 flights of stairs—805 steps, 515 feet, AUL helped the Indy Runners Club organize the first AUL Stairclimb, an event that has since become best known as the "Bop to the Top." When organizations wanted a new place for an art exhibit, an orchid show, or some other type of program, the building's atrium lobby and adjoining auditorium were made available.

When employees were asked by a writer for the AULnews how they liked working downtown, most called it "enjoyable" or "exciting." And when residents of Indianapolis were surveyed by Walker Research, Inc., in 1984, most (54.7 percent) said they knew about AUL because of the new building.

Looking back on that period now, Chairman Jerry Semler said he felt that the AUL Tower provided much of the leverage that started the redevelopment of downtown Indianapolis. Former Indianapolis Mayor William H. Hudnut III agreed (see sidebar on facing page).

But all the good things being said about the new building didn't help the company's performance a whole lot at first since the early 1980s were marked by a sluggish economy and high interest rates, and the insurance industry was in a period of rapid change and intense competition.

"Today, change comes on with all the energy of a rampaging bull," AUL's field force was told by Jack B. Turner, CLU, president of the Million Dollar Round Table (MDRT) and a speaker at the Celebration Indy '83 business conference. "There must have been more change in our industry during my forty months on the executive committee [of MDRT], than possibly during the past forty years of our industry."

John Barbre, CLU, senior vice president for marketing at AUL, told the same gathering, "The life insurance industry has moved from a high profit margin business to a low profit margin business in the last few years. I would think it would be a severe mistake for any insurance company to think that it is still operating in the era of high margins of profit."

New products, highly competitive products, had become a necessity, and AUL worked hard to stay competitive. In 1983 the company introduced American Universal Life, a hot new individual life product featuring flexible premiums and flexible protection plans. It introduced ComPac I and II, new group life and health medical plans with cost-containment features to help offset the soaring cost of health care. And, in its newly created pension division, AUL made product enhancements and service improvements in an effort to keep pace in this fast-changing marketplace.

In response to the rapid increase in interest rates and in policy loans, the company introduced a market loan rate provision under which policy loan interest rates would fluctuate with interest rates in the rest of the economy. With the market loan rate came the prospect of higher dividends for policyowners. The market loan rate was contained in all new policies, and existing policyowners were given a chance to convert to it and qualify for significantly higher dividends.

These efforts paid off quickly. In 1984 American Universal Life outsold all of the company's other personal life products, and in 1985 it accounted for more than half of the company's business in the individual line, with sales

Bop to the Top participants race one at a time up the 805 steps of the AUL Tower. The winners usually finish in four to five minutes, but with several hundred participants, the event usually takes more than two hours to complete.

Determination and heart are what count. Bop to the Top is open to participants of all ages. Don Carr of the Tuxedo Brothers, which stages the event each year, said he has seen racers as young as four years old and as old as eighty.

Many of the Boppers need a little assistance by the time they reach the thirty-seventh floor, but the sense of accomplishment seems to bring many of them back year after year.

increasing 72 percent over the previous year. All the product divisions were profitable and several sales records were set in 1984 and again in 1985.

In its 1984 annual report, AUL reported: "From its founding in 1877, it took the company 101 years to reach $1 billion in assets and 102 years to reach $10 billion of insurance in force. Then it took only six years to get the second billion in assets and only five years to double that $10 billion of life insurance in force. The company has also been able to double its surplus (capital) in the last six years, reaching $100,399,656 at the end of 1984."

By 1984 the AUL Tower was a recognized landmark in downtown Indianapolis. The AUL signboards, with their puns and topical quips, were re-established on two corners of the employee parking lot on the block north of the building. And the company was becoming more involved in the community around it.

That first AUL Stairclimb in February 1984 drew 683 participants, 563 of whom made it to the thirty-seventh floor finish line. The winner, Mark Carlson, a twenty-one-year-old cyclist, weightlifter, and member of the Butler University track team, bounded up the 805 steps in four minutes and five seconds. The top female finisher, Patricia Hagen, an *Indianapolis Star* reporter, did the climb in five minutes and fifty-six seconds. Proceeds from the race went to the Leukemia Society. The Bop to the Top has become an annual event at the AUL Tower, and it is now a fundraiser for Riley Hospital for Children.

A month after that first Stairclimb, AUL joined with Indiana Governor Robert Orr to start the first AUL/Governor's Cup Running Series. This was a series of ten eight-kilometer [five-mile] road races in cities around Indiana. The final race of the series, in downtown Indianapolis, began on Capitol Avenue in front of the Indiana Statehouse and finished on Ohio Street in front of the AUL Tower. More than twelve hundred runners participated in that finale, which was won by Bill Rodgers in twenty-four minutes and twenty-six seconds. Rodgers is the only four-time winner of the New York City and Boston Marathons.

On the two days preceding that event, AUL and the Governor's Health Project sponsored "Healthfest '84" in the lobby of the AUL Tower, where more than a thousand people visited booths set up by forty health services agencies. Free health screenings and information on physical fitness were provided at the exhibits. The following year, and for seven more years, all the AUL/Governor's Cup events except the finale were held in Indiana State Parks. The finale was always held in downtown Indianapolis. The series was discontinued in 1992.

Personal computers began to show up in AUL agency offices and in the home office in 1984. In January 1984, there were only four IBM personal computers in the company's field force, all part of a highly touted program to see if PCs would meet the needs of the agents. By January 1985, there were 115 PCs in 42 AUL agencies around the country. There were also eighteen in the home office and eight in AUL regional sales offices. There were requests for many more. By 1986 all of AUL's general agencies and regional sales offices

The AUL/Governor's Cup Series was begun by AUL and Indiana Governor Robert Orr to promote health and fitness and attracted thousands of participants each year. Held as a benefit for the Indiana State Parks, except for the first year, the regional events of the series were held in those parks. The final race of each year's series started at the east steps of the Indiana State House and finished in front of the AUL Tower. More than 2,000 runners and 600 walkers took part in this finale on September 24, 1988.

Bill Rodgers, the only four-time winner of both the Boston and New York Marathons, twice participated in the finale of the AUL/Governor's Cup Series. He won the inaugural event in 1984 and he returned in 1988, when he wore the number forty and set a new world's record for people over forty years of age competing in an eight-kilometer race.

As many as fifty agencies and organizations had booths at Healthfest, a two-day health fair that was held in the lobby of the AUL Tower each September preceding the AUL/Governor's Cup finale. Screening tests and information on a wide range of health and fitness subjects were provided.

"Blow as hard as you can" was the direction given people taking this pulmonary function test at Healthfest. AUL employees were encouraged to participate in the health fairs, which were also open to the public free of charge.

were linked with the home office through a system of PCs and special leased-line telephone service, all part of the Direct Access Remote Terminals (DART) Network.

In 1985 the pension division also purchased and began installing a major new computer system called MAAS—Multiple Account Annuity System—that would eventually give AUL the technology, speed, and flexibility needed as a major competitor in the pension field. And that same year, the company completed a new corporate identity program and introduced a sleek red-and-blue AUL logo. The new design had the modern look that fit this fast-growing company, and the colors were most appropriate for a company with "American" in its name and a huge American flag flying from the top of its home office.

In 1987 AUL underwent an internal reorganization, creating four completely separate product divisions—individual, group, pension, and reinsurance. Each product division developed its own five-year strategic plan to deal with what Semler called a "product revolution" in the industry. "We went from being a functional company to one with four business units where the senior officer in each of the divisions had total responsibility for revenue, pricing and administration," Semler said. "It worked very well because at the same time we had the philosophy of sustainable growth, where we managed our capital and held our senior officers accountable for growing only as fast as capital would allow."

Since the original "King Kong," there has been some association of gorillas and tall buildings, but motorists surely were a bit surprised one morning to see this 40-foot, 300-pound inflatable gorilla on the side of the AUL Tower holding a sign saying "AUL goes ape over the new zoo." This was AUL's way of helping promote the new zoo in White River State Park, which opened to the public June 11, 1988.

As the 1980s progressed, AUL continued to do well, except in the ever-changing area of health insurance. In the 1988 annual report, Chairman Jack Reich and President Jerry Semler wrote:

"For American United Life, 1988 was a year of tremendous growth, with new sales records set in a number of areas. . . . A lot of the satisfaction that came from these achievements, however, was offset by concern over our losses in group health insurance. These losses occurred despite large rate increases imposed during the year. We were not the only ones to have trouble with the group health product. More than 80 percent of the companies selling health insurance lost money on that line of business in 1987 and there is every indication that the nationwide experience was even worse in 1988 as medical costs escalated and the use of health insurance by individuals increased."

In 1986, the company introduced a new logo in block-style red and blue, similar to the colors in the American flag. The logo was designed by Crosby Associates of Chicago, and became the fifth corporate logo for AUL since 1936.

The company cut back in the health area and revised its medical products each year as it tried to find a profitable solution, but the situation continued to be a challenge until, in the early 1990s, the company got out of the health insurance business altogether. In the 1994 annual report, Semler wrote:

"The current environment, with constantly rising claim costs, makes these health insurance products neither viable nor profitable for all but the largest health insurance providers, and the capital previously committed to these marginal lines of business will now be available to allow us to focus on our strengths in other lines of business."

In 1987, while AUL was still dealing with the health insurance problem, the stock market crashed, and in 1990 the country began to slip into a recession. Some insurance companies were having serious financial problems. AUL continued to do well, but it had to respond to the national concern, repeatedly reassuring its policyowners, clients and prospective clients that it was a sound company that placed a high priority on maintaining its financial strength. That message was well stated in AUL's 1990 annual report. It said in part:

> Most of AUL's assets, like those of any insurance company, are invested and held as reserves to pay future benefits. Profits the company earns are put in our policyowners' capital and surplus accounts. These funds become our operating capital and our safety margin for unforeseen economic losses.
>
> The quality of our assets is one of the company's greatest strengths. By being very selective, we have been able to maintain a mortgage loan portfolio that provides a high yield and virtually no payment delinquencies, making it one of the best mortgage loan portfolios in the industry. Our bond portfolio also has an outstanding record in comparison with the industry. The company has always steered away from so-called junk bonds. Diversification by maturity, geography, industry and company is closely scrutinized.
>
> Size and strength in the insurance industry are not necessarily synonymous. And with our philosophy and our highly disciplined

investment process, we at AUL have always sought to be a tower of strength for our policyowners and clients. In each of the last two years, AUL has had a record-setting net gain from operations. Much of this has been used to build financial strength. Our policyowners' capital and surplus accounts have increased by more than 30 percent in the last two years to a total of $214.8 million. . . .

We have been weathering the economic storms for more than 113 years, and we believe we have the right people, the right products and the financial strength to keep weathering them in the years ahead.

Based on the company's financial condition and operating performance, AUL was rated A-plus (superior) by the A. M. Best Company, the leading independent analyst of the insurance industry, and it had had Best's top rating or the equivalent recommendation since 1950. But the recession and the financial problems being experienced by some financial institutions at that time caused many persons to continue to question the financial soundness of banks, savings and loan associations, and insurance companies with which they did business. Ratings became the common measure of financial strength. So, in 1991, AUL sought ratings of its claim-paying ability from two major credit rating companies, Duff & Phelps, Inc., and Standard & Poor's Corporation.

Both rating companies put AUL in the excellent category. Duff & Phelps gave AUL a rating of AA-plus, the second highest of nineteen rating levels, and Standard & Poor's rated the company AA-minus, the fourth highest of twenty-two levels. By Standard & Poor's definition, insurers with a rating in the AA category "offer excellent financial security, and their capacity to meet

Chairman Jack Reich was honored in 1990 with a lifetime achievement award for community service from the Indiana Council of Fund Raising Executives. The award was presented by the state's first lady, Susan Bayh, who also presented Reich with a Sagamore of the Wabash from Governor Evan Bayh, the fifth Indiana governor to name Reich a Sagamore of the Wabash. Mrs. Reich is on the right. In 1991, Reich was inducted into the Central Indiana Business Hall of Fame established by Junior Achievement.

policyholder obligations differs only in a small degree from insurers rated AAA." Standard & Poor's said AUL's rating of AA-minus "reflects its market position in group pensions, good overall profitability, low investment risk and conservative capitalization."

Duff & Phelps said its AA-plus rating recognizes AUL's "superior quality investments, its significant presence in the . . . group annuity market, the benefits of reorganizational efforts in recent years which have substantially improved management and cost controls, and the ability of the company to produce an above average return on adjusted surplus while maintaining a degree of operating leverage appropriate for its business mix." Later, Moody's Investors Service rated AUL A1 (good).

Jim Shanahan, senior vice president of the pension division at the time, who had been one of the leading advocates of the additional ratings, said, "Other companies who were in the pension business were getting ratings over and above Best. Best, in and of itself, didn't matter. We were being asked what our ratings were. It became a sales hindrance." And he said the additional ratings proved valuable in boosting pension sales in the years that followed.

On April 1, 1989, Jack Reich stepped down as chief executive officer, relinquishing that responsibility to Jerry Semler. On August 31, 1991, Reich retired and Semler became chairman of the board as well as CEO and president. Reich, who had been a director since 1957 and chairman since 1967, was named an honorary director and chairman emeritus. He died September 26, 1996, at the age of eighty-six.

Like the building he built and the company he led for twenty-four years, Jack Reich had been a tower of strength.

During much of his term as vice president of the United States, Hoosier Dan Quayle had an office in the AUL Tower—Suite 1600. It was opened in July 1989 but, for security reasons, there was very little publicity, not even a nameplate on the front door. Before the vice president could move in, bulletproof glass was put in the windows and special security systems installed in the walls, ceiling, and floor. Quayle's staff used the office more than he did, but on a visit in November 1989, Quayle addressed AUL employees and building tenants from a special platform set up in the building's courtyard. Standing behind Quayle at that event are (from left) Chairman Jack Reich; Alice Davidson and Robert Rowe, who staffed Quayle's Indianapolis office, and Marilyn Tucker Quayle.

This view of the courtyard of the AUL Tower was the first painting done for AUL by Artist Harry Davis. It was commissioned by the AUL board of directors and presented to Jack Reich in recognition of more than twenty-one years as the company's chief executive officer. Reich stepped down as CEO on April 1, 1989.

CHAPTER 10

THE 1990s — WHAT A DECADE!

There was a time in America when a good small insurance company could prosper, and AUL did. Back in the 1950s, Clarence Jackson was fond of saying AUL wasn't good because it was old, it was old because over the years it had been a good company. Later, Jack Reich said he didn't seek to build a big company, he sought to make AUL a quality company. And he did that.

But by the 1990s, Jerry Semler spoke frequently of the importance of achieving "critical mass." That was vital, and a company now needed some size to achieve the low unit costs that are the essence of critical mass. Low unit costs had become extremely important for two reasons: competition and technology.

Competition in the insurance industry had become progressively more intense as financial institutions grew, diversified, and went high tech. To be competitive in the industry in the 1990s, companies had to invest millions of dollars in ever-changing computer hardware and software. The technology allowed them to design, sell and service more sophisticated products faster, better and over greater distances. But to keep the prices of those products competitive, they had to be able to spread those ever-rising costs over more and more sales. In other words, they had to grow. They had to achieve critical mass. And to do that required ever-increasing amounts of money.

Those were the forces that influenced the reshaping of American United Life Insurance Company during the last decade of the twentieth century.

Achieving critical mass means making sure that each product line—and every product within that line—brings in enough revenue to cover the costs involved in developing, marketing and servicing that product. AUL's Executive Vice President Steve Radcliffe characterized it as a balancing act. "As long as there is a right balance between the amount of revenue coming in and the bills that we have to pay to keep the place open," Radcliffe said, "I think we have critical mass." That balance can be achieved by increasing revenue or controlling costs, or both.

The reality, however, was that AUL needed to grow. Semler said, "What influences the growth and critical mass concept is the ever-increasing cost of technology. I think technology's bar gets raised every year, and we have to figure a way to continue to leverage the technology throughout the enterprise to get our unit cost down. We have got to keep growing."

AUL entered the nineties in good financial shape, and in 1990, when many companies were struggling, AUL had a record high net income of $28.5 million. Even group health insurance was profitable after five straight years of losses. In 1991 the company had net income of $30.8 million—another record—and more than $1 billion in total revenue for the first time ever. In 1992 it had net income of $22.1 million and passed $5 billion in assets.

The company grew in the nineties—in a number of different ways—and it did well throughout the decade. In 1990 AUL acquired most of the failing Life of Indiana Insurance Company, which added more than sixty-four hundred policyholders. In 1992 it spent $7 million to purchase a block of new reinsurance business and to purchase the life insurance business of Mutual Security Life Insurance Company of Fort Wayne. The right to buy the Mutual Security business was awarded by the state after it took over the floundering company. AUL had earlier signed contracts with many Mutual Security agents, allowing them to sell AUL products. In 1993 the company added nine new agencies.

In 1990 the company also added a very popular new feature to the AUL Tower, a ninety-seven-hundred-square-foot fitness center, operated by personnel from the National Institute for Fitness and Sport. Membership in the center was open to all tenants in the building, as well as to members of the Skyline Club. AUL paid part of its employees' dues and allowed them to pay the balance through payroll deduction.

Members were able to begin using the fitness center May 10, 1990, but the grand opening—and it was grand—took place in late September. On September 24 about 350 people crowded into the center to see members of the President's Council on Physical Fitness and Sport. They were in Indianapolis

Jerry D. Semler was elected chairman of the board of directors of American United Life Insurance Company in 1991 following the retirement of Jack Reich. Semler also retained the positions of president and chief executive officer.

for a meeting, and Dr. Cory SerVaas, a Council member from Indianapolis, arranged for the group to help AUL dedicate its new fitness center. Reed Engel, the center director, was the master of ceremonies, but actor Arnold Schwarzenegger, chairman of the President's Council, stole the show when he christened the new facility with a stage-prop champagne bottle filled with confetti. The center had sports celebrity guests all that week, but Schwarzenegger proved the star attraction.

During the last decade of the twentieth century, the year 1994 was particularly notable. That year AUL stopped selling individual and group major medical policies. "It was a hard decision to make at the time, but it was the right decision," Chairman Semler said. "We didn't have the critical size." That same year, AUL purchased the individual and group disability business of Educators Mutual Life Insurance Company of Lancaster, Pennsylvania. This action added 20,000 individual life policies and group disability contracts

Arnold Schwarzenegger, then chairman of the President's Council on Physical Fitness and Sports, helped open the AUL Tower Fitness Center on September 24, 1990. He and others on the Council, who were in town at the invitation of Council member Dr. Cory SerVaas of Indianapolis, were among 350 people who crowded into the fitness center for the ceremony.

Schwarzenegger made the opening official by smashing a confetti-filled champagne bottle. Reed Engel (behind Schwarzenegger), the first director of the fitness center, served as master of ceremonies for the ceremony.

covering 25,000 people. The company also entered into what it called "a strategic alliance" with The State Life Insurance Company of Indianapolis. It also added eleven new agencies and nine new regional group and pension sales offices around the country. And it introduced an individual variable annuity, the first of an AUL line of variable products for individuals.

In announcing its purchase of the Educators Mutual Life disability business, AUL said the action was taken to spread administrative expense and help amortize the company's investment in new technology. Under its alliance with State Life, AUL said it would handle most of State Life's administrative functions, but both companies would maintain their separate identities and separate distribution systems, which would lower costs and add market capabilities for both companies.

AUL set company records in 1994 for premium income and pre-tax net gain. Premium income was $759.2 million, up 17 percent over 1993, making the year one of the best ever for premium growth. Despite its investment in the Educators Mutual business, AUL's pretax net gain was $55.5 million, up $5 million from 1993. Net income was $28 million.

There was no new record in net income in 1994 only because of a 33 percent jump in taxes, but in 1995 AUL's net income rose 56.8 percent and set a new company record of $41.9 million. Life insurance in force reached a record high of $74.1 billion, and assets increased to $6.5 billion. The pension division set sales records in 1995, and sales of AUL's individual variable annuity (IVA) took off in its first full year on the market. Six new investment options had been added, giving IVA customers a total of eighteen investment options.

In 1996 net income was $52.1 million, assets passed $7 billion, and growth continued as all four product divisions did well. During the year, AUL purchased a block of group long-term disability (LTD) business from National Insurance Services (NIS) of Wisconsin and became the preferred carrier for future group LTD business written by the Schools Insurance Fund Trust, which NIS markets and administers.

That same year AUL formed AUL International as the reinsurance division entered into reinsurance contracts with several insurers in Europe and made plans to establish new partnerships in Central and South America. The company also became a bigger player in the accident and health reinsurance market by becoming an equity partner in Reinsurance Services of Princeton (RSP), in Princeton, New Jersey.

The reinsurance division was part of an industry first in November 1996 when Northwestern Mutual Life Insurance Company sent, and AUL received, computerized encrypted data that reduced the need for exchange of paper on a reinsurance case. That year also AUL made its first appearance on the Internet at **www.aul.com**.

A company's success is usually measured in numbers, but the life insurance business is a business with a passion for helping individuals, families, and businesses, and almost as frequently as he talks about critical mass, Jerry Semler talks about the importance of the company's fundamental values. So, in the middle of the successful nineties, AUL took time to restate its fundamental values—achievement, stewardship, partnership, integrity, responsiveness and excellence—in an acronym, ASPIRE, which it promoted to employees, agents, and customers.

"As our company grew," Semler said, "we wanted to be sure everyone was on the same page, that we all had the same values and knew that corporate culture is important . . . and I think ASPIRE has helped guide us."

In 1997 AUL achieved membership in the Insurance Marketplace Standards Association, which promotes high standards of ethical behavior in the marketplace. To qualify, AUL underwent a self-analysis and independent third-party assessments. The company had net income of $74.3 million in 1997. Total revenue was up 13.3 percent to $1.1 billion, assets were up 10 percent to $8.5 billion, and the average net yield on invested assets was 8.02 percent—nearly half a percentage point above the industry average. Pension assets under management exceeded $5 billion for the first time.

AUL entered into a strategic alliance with Indianapolis Life Insurance Company in 1997, but both companies had reservation about the arrangement and it was discontinued some months later. AUL also entered into an alliance with Pioneer Mutual Life Insurance Company, a 130-year-old company based in Fargo, North Dakota. That relationship has lasted.

With its new alliances, AUL began talking about bringing its affiliated companies together in a mutual holding company structure. AUL lobbied in the 1998 and 1999 sessions of the Indiana General Assembly to get a mutual holding company law, under which the company could reorganize as a stock company under a mutual holding company umbrella. That legislation was

R. Stephen Radcliffe, AUL's executive vice president, has been with the company since 1977 and has been a member of the board of directors since 1991. A Fellow of the Society of Actuaries (FSA) and a Chartered Life Underwriter (CLU), he is a former chief actuary of the company. He is also a past president of the Society of Actuaries.

signed into law by Governor Frank O'Bannon on December 1, 1999. AUL immediately sought, and received, policyowner approval to proceed with the reorganization.

"The reason that we thought this mutual holding company concept would be the best for us," Executive Vice President Steve Radcliffe said, "is that it allowed us to combine with both mutual companies and with stock companies under one common umbrella. If we had fully demutualized, we would become a stock company totally. We would convert all policyholders into stockholders. And then each company we brought in—for instance, State Life—would have to demutualize, turn all its policyholders into stockholders. It's very expensive to do that. It's three, four, five times as expensive as just bringing them in as a mutual company. So this structure gives us the flexibility to combine with other mutual companies. It also gives us the flexibility of buying companies. The mutual holding company can buy stock companies as well. So we felt it was the best of both worlds. And then there is the special kicker that we get to save a tax bill of about $6 million a year as a side benefit. So, all these things came together to make our board say that in order to be positioned for the

Applause greeted Indiana Governor Frank O'Bannon's signing of the insurance mutual holding company bill into law on December 1, 1999. The signing ceremony was attended by a group of legislators and insurance industry leaders who had worked hard to obtain passage of the measure, which the Indiana General Assembly passed, after much delay, on November 23.

future, to give us the extra flexibility that we needed, we should make the conversion now."

An added benefit of the mutual holding company structure is that it would allow AUL to raise capital by issuing stock, something both Semler and Radcliffe say is not likely to happen in the foreseeable future. An advantage the mutual holding company structure has over straight demutualization is that another stock company cannot come along and take over AUL. "We want to remain independent, headquartered here, and continuing our strategy of growing and serving people," Semler said. "If we totally demutualized, we'd be gone. We'd disappear."

In 1998 AUL began to develop an electronic business strategy as the Internet became an increasingly important factor in the servicing of the types of sophisticated insurance and investment products that AUL was selling. In 1999 the pension division's NetServe became an interactive Web site providing participants with transactional capabilities as well as information about their accounts. In addition, the individual division had its Online Services and the group division had www.employeebenefits.aul.com. The pension division also had a Web site for retirement plan sponsors, and it was continually adding enhancements to TeleServe, its interactive voice response system.

The reinsurance division, which had already been a pioneer in electronic data transfer, went in a couple of new directions. After venturing into Central and South America in 1997 in search of reinsurance business, it opened its first branch office in Buenos Aires, Argentina, in 1999. The main office of AUL International is in Coral Gables, Florida. Also in 1999, AUL bought the accident and long-term care divisions of reinsurer Duncanson and Holt from UnumProvident Insurance Company and created AUL Reinsurance Man-

John R. Barton became senior vice president for the group division on December 31, 1998, succeeding Gerald T. Walker, who retired after serving in that position since 1990. Barton is also president of CNL Financial Corporation and Cherokee National Life Insurance Company, companies acquired by AUL on December 18, 2000. In part through its acquisition of Cherokee National, AUL greatly increased its position in the credit life and disability markets. As a result of a relationship with R. E. Moulton, a managing general underwriter based in Marblehead, Massachusetts, it has also aggressively grown its medical stop-loss business in the last two years. AUL continues to be a provider of traditional and voluntary group life and disability insurance.

agement Services (RMS). That action made AUL one of the nation's leading reinsurance carriers of accident and long-term care coverage. Despite these purchases, AUL's net income in 1999 was $68.2 million, up 2.6 percent over 1998. Assets in 1999 went from $9.3 billion to $10.6 billion, and life insurance in force increased from $133.1 billion to $167.2 billion.

Of course, 1999 was also the year everyone was talking, and worrying, about what was called "the Y2K problem." What would happen to all the computers and the computer-run operations when the calendar rolled from 1999 to 2000, people wondered. By the 1990s practically everything AUL did depended on a computer, and as AUL's senior vice president and chief information officer at the time, Scott Kincaid, said, "insurance processing by its nature is date sensitive." So, for AUL, work on the Y2K problem began in 1996, and by 1999 the company was ready—but still nervous about what might happen at midnight on New Year's Eve. "The good news is we were over-prepared," Kincaid said. The biggest technology project AUL ever undertook—spanning four years, involving at least five hundred people at one time or another, and costing $18.1 million—was a success. All the systems continued to work, and AUL rolled smoothly into Year 2000.

What a decade it had been for AUL! At the end of 1989, after 112 years in business, AUL had assets of almost $3.7 billion. At the end of 1999, after 122 years, assets were $10.6 billion. At the beginning of the decade, the company had $33.3 billion of life insurance in force. At the end of the decade, the face value of life insurance in force was $167.2 billion. Total revenue in 1989 was $846.9 million. Total revenue in 1999 was $1.546 billion. Net income in 1989 was almost $26 million. Ten years later, it had risen to $68.2 million. And, possibly the most significant figures of all, total capital increased from $195.1 million in 1989 to $739.2 million in 1999.

Year 2000 was another growth year, with life insurance in force increasing significantly to $201 billion. Assets grew to $10.9 billion, with net income up 17.6 percent to $80.3 million. Furthermore, capital, the foundation of the company's strength, was up 14.7 percent for the year to $847.6 million—four times what it had been a decade earlier.

Why was it such a strong decade of growth? "I think we were strategically positioned with our 401(k) business," Semler said. "Today that represents about 53 percent of our revenue, deposits in the 401(k), 457 and 403(b) accounts. It was a strong period of growth in the economy, it fueled the stock market, and we were well positioned with daily account valuation to be able to get a jump start on the market and the explosion of the 401(k)." Radcliffe agreed, adding, "We did a good job because, I think, if there is anything that this company does well, at the top of the list has to be investments. Our investment department has continually earned high return with low risk."

No mention of critical mass, but, obviously, as a company, AUL was achieving it during that last decade of the century.

A 20-by-38-foot American flag, one of those usually flown atop the AUL Tower, is traditionally displayed in the building's atrium lobby each year from Flag Day to the Fourth of July. It was also displayed during Operation Desert Storm and was put up again following the terrorists' attacks of September 11, 2001. Chairman Jerry Semler said he wanted the flag left up for one year in memory of those who died in those attacks.

In 1982 Dr. John Pearson, who coordinated AUL's move downtown, referred to the pick-up and drop-off lane on the north side of the building as "the kissing lane." The name caught on with employees, and in 1992, Edmund Genier (right), AUL's vice president for real estate, with the assistance of Terry Meinders, one of the building maintenance staff, erected this sign, making the name official.

CHAPTER 11

A REINSURANCE PIONEER

Elijah B. Martindale, the first president of American Central, and Charles E. Dark, the company's vice president and superintendent of agencies, made a major decision in 1904 that helped shape the future of American United Life. They decided their company should go into the reinsurance business.

By 2001 AUL was the eighth largest life reinsurer in North America, and the oldest domestic life reinsurer in the United States.

Reinsurance is insurance on insurance. After selling a life insurance policy to an individual, particularly if it is for a large amount, the insuring company often gets another company or companies to share in that risk. Those companies become the reinsurers. They accept part of the risk and receive part of the premium. Reinsurance makes it possible for even very small companies to compete in the marketplace for policies that might otherwise be beyond their capacity.

The first reinsurance agreement American Central signed in 1904 was with The State Life Insurance Company of Indianapolis and, under that agreement, it assumed $5,000 of the risk on a $10,000 policy written on the life of an Indianapolis man.

In those early days, Major Carroll B. Carr, secretary and actuary for American Central, did much of the traveling, calling on other insurance companies and returning with new reinsurance agreements.

"Major Carr was one of the most popular men in western life insurance," Wendell P. Coler later wrote in a review of the reinsurance department. Coler had joined American Central in 1932 as an actuary. "When Major Carr died," he wrote, "[President Herbert] Woollen immediately took steps to bring Harry R. Wilson, a boyhood friend then engaged in the contracting business in Chicago, into the company. The first reinsurance contract that Wilson executed on behalf of the company was with O. J. Arnold and the Illinois Life. At the end of 1919 when separate statistics for reinsurance operations were maintained, reinsurance in force was over $20 million. During the boom period of the twenties, it increased to $133 million."

Henry Buttolph, who had handled some reinsurance business for the company after Carr died, apparently disliked train travel, so when Wilson said he was willing to go calling alone, he got the chance. In fact, President Woollen had been grooming him for the job.

In a 1967 interview, Woollen said, "For months I had been preparing him for the job and he didn't recognize it. He didn't know anything about insurance, so I was surprised when he came into my office to tell me good-bye when he started on his first trip. I asked who was going with him and he said 'no one.' I asked what he would do if he met technical questions about insurance and he said he would manage. If the answer was needed in a hurry, he would make some excuse, go to the telephone, and call the company for the answer. If he had more time, he would telegraph for it." Woollen described Wilson as "a nervy fellow."

Wilson, a graduate engineer, took to the reinsurance business and traveled for many years, making friends with insurance company presidents all over the nation. It is reported that he once asked a Pullman porter, "How many sleeping cars do you have in operation?" "Oh, about a thousand, I reckon," the porter answered. "I thought so," Wilson responded, "and I've slept in every one of them." Wilson, who headed the reinsurance operations from 1918 to 1953,

American Central's reinsurance department in 1931. Harry R. Wilson (standing) headed the company's reinsurance operations from 1918 to 1953.

also became a major stockholder and director of American Central. He served on the board of AUL until 1967. In his obituary, he was described as "instrumental in developing AUL as one of the life insurance industry's foremost reinsurers."

Upon the merger of American Central and United Mutual at the end of 1936, American Central had $78,575,463 in reinsurance in force and $76,215,476 in direct business.

H. Hartzell Perry joined American Central in 1938 and rose to become a long-time vice president for reinsurance. He said the reinsurance business slowed down during the Depression, but in 1952, the new president, Clarence Jackson, told the reinsurance department "to take off and run," and the company was soon doing twice as much reinsurance business as direct business.

When interviewed in 1967, Perry said, "It is rather common to have a $1 million policy, and I recall a $5 million policy. In the course of reinsurance, AUL has joined in policies on the lives of Elizabeth Taylor, Tom Mix, Mae West, and Rudolph Valentino, to name a few I can remember." (Today, the company's privacy policy would not permit such disclosures.)

Perry went on to say, "reinsurance contracts and rates are pretty much alike [from company to company]. Companies look for service and for people they

The reinsurance department in 1957. H. Hartzell Perry (standing in center aisle at back) headed the department at that time.

can trust. You have to build partnerships and loyalty, keep on your toes and continue [to provide] service." That description is still true today.

In 1959 AUL's reinsurance department began sponsoring executive workshops for top-echelon officers of insurance companies from across the nation. These dealt with such topics as company management, new developments in the industry, investments, variable annuities, mutual funds and health insurance.

For years, the highly popular workshops were held annually, often at exotic vacation resorts. They were very successful and widely praised for their education and stimulation of newer company personnel. In 1966, the Indiana state insurance commissioner, Joseph Wood, called AUL's executive workshops "a contribution to the whole life insurance industry."

During the 1970s and 1980s, under the leadership of Rodney R. Petterson, who headed the reinsurance division from 1969 to 1987, the division grew rapidly. During the decade of the 1970s, sales tripled. In 1969 the face value of new life reinsurance sold by AUL was $495 million. Ten years later, it was $1.5 billion. Insurance in force went from $1.7 billion in 1969 to $4.9 billion in 1979. Then in 1980, the company had more than $2 billion of new reinsurance sales—a company record at the time.

To sustain its growth, however, AUL had to adjust to an ever-changing market. The formation of new insurance companies nearly ceased by 1970, and those new, small companies had been a prime reinsurance market for AUL. When that market faded, AUL redirected its focus to larger companies, a market that was growing. Over time, the company also had to adjust its marketing strategies, but the ever-popular executive workshops were not abandoned.

Taking a lunch break at a September 1966 executive workshop held in Indianapolis are (from left around table) Kenneth K. S. Fong, Pacific Guardian Life; Herbert M. Gomez, Royal State National; E. M. Karrmann, AUL president; Mrs. Herbert Gomez; Hartzell Perry, AUL vice president for reinsurance; and Sid Collins, Indianapolis radio personality and voice of the Indianapolis 500 Mile Race for many years. Collins was a speaker at the workshop.

The executive workshops became known as Partnership Forums, which were held every other year. Charles D. Lineback, senior vice president for reinsurance, said, "People's time is so important today. This schedule seems to work better for everyone. We focus in on trying to get the key decision-makers at companies that are already clients of ours as well as our top prospects."

Lineback joined AUL in 1969 and became a part of the reinsurance division in 1975. He became head of that division when Rodney Petterson retired. Lineback was named senior vice president for reinsurance in 1988. Under his leadership, the division experienced tremendous growth, expanding into new fields and into foreign markets.

In 1988 the reinsurance division began covering accident and health lines of business, and, not long after, it began to participate in a form of reinsurance called pooled reinsurance. "It was non-life reinsurance," Lineback said, "mostly accident and health, some LTD [long-term disability]. This was offered to reinsurers through reinsurance pools. There were two or three dominant pool managers in the United States at that time. Our philosophy was to align ourselves with the top ones and grow more in that business. The two leads were Duncanson and Holt and Reinsurance Management Services, or RMS as it was referred to. And that was quite successful from its beginning."

When UnumProvident Corporation bought Duncanson and Holt and Duncanson and Holt in turn purchased RMS, AUL's opportunities in this field began to shrink. But in 1996 when a key executive of Duncanson and Holt went out on his own and formed Reinsurance Services of Princeton (RSP), AUL saw a new opportunity and bought an equity position in RSP.

"They began to write new business," Lineback said, "and we formed pools with AUL being the lead, and it worked fairly well. Then in April of 1999 an

Charles D. Lineback succeeded Rod Petterson as head of AUL's reinsurance division in 1987. He was named senior vice president, reinsurance, in 1988. In 1999, he was also elected president and chief executive officer of AUL Reinsurance Management Services.

announcement was made by Unum that they were going to sell Duncanson and Holt, which intrigued us very much because they were much larger than RSP."

AUL began negotiating with UnumProvident and in August, 1999 agreed to buy portions of Duncanson and Holt. "We bought just what fit into our plans," Lineback said, "and that was the accident division and the long-term care division. . . . They had eight offices. We reduced that to three. They had in total 175 people. We reduced that to 125 people. What we ended up with was a very strong organization."

The new operation was called AUL Reinsurance Management Services (RMS). Lineback added to his credentials the title of president of AUL RMS, with offices in Princeton, New Jersey; New York City, and Avon, Connecticut. In addition to Indianapolis, AUL RMS has satellite offices in Toronto, Seattle and San Francisco, which market all of AUL's reinsurance products.

Also, in 1997 AUL created an international operation based in Coral Gables, Florida, near Miami, and began offering reinsurance services in Central and South America. In November 1999 it opened its first branch office in Buenos Aires, Argentina.

The reinsurance division pioneered in developing and using technology to reduce the need for paper transactions, and in November 1996 the company was part of an industry first when Northwestern Mutual Life Insurance Company sent, and AUL received, computerized encrypted data that reduced the need for exchange of paper on a reinsurance case. Because of its work in this area, AUL was asked to serve on the American National Standards Institute committee that has since set the standards needed to enable the industry to maximize the use of electronic data interchange.

Michael Barnett joined AUL as a member of the reinsurance division in 1979. As vice president of that section, Barnett ran the entire North American life reinsurance operation under Lineback. Barnett is active on a number of industry committees, including the American Council of Life Insurance reinsurance committee.

AUL's commitment to partnership was the theme of this reinsurance promotional piece from the early 1990s.

Europe is the birthplace of reinsurance, and all of the world's largest reinsurers are there, but AUL was the eighth largest life reinsurer in North America by the end of 2001. Because of its recent acquisitions, Lineback added, "we became the largest reinsurer of long-term care in North America—by a wide margin, I might add—and we also became one of the leading accident reinsurers in North America, one of the top three."

In addition, because reinsurance generates a large volume of insurance in force, AUL has traditionally had more insurance in force than many life insurance companies that are larger when measured by assets, employees, or other criteria.

During the year 2001, as the insurance industry continued its rapid change toward financial services, and small-to-medium-sized companies found it particularly important to carve out niche markets, AUL reevaluated its long-term business plans. In doing so, it was decided that the company needed to sharpen its focus on its core direct insurance and retirement plan businesses to benefit its policyholders in the most effective way. At the August 2001 board of directors meeting, the company was given approval to seek a reinsurance partner who would ultimately take over AUL's reinsurance operations over the next few years. Effectively, the company would be exiting the reinsurance business in order to focus on the three direct product lines—individual operations, retirement services, and group operations.

Employers Re (ERC), a subsidiary of General Electric, was selected by AUL to indemnity reinsure AUL's life, long-term care, and international blocks of reinsurance business. As part of the transaction, many of AUL's eighty-four Indianapolis-based life reinsurance employees were offered opportunities to join ERC, which will maintain operations in Indianapolis.

"Much of the value of this business is based in the knowledge and experience of our people," Jerry Semler said. "One of the primary reasons ERC was selected to reinsure this business is that they value the knowledge and capabilities the existing AUL reinsurance employees bring with them. . . . AUL recognizes and appreciates the contributions these people have made to the company throughout their respective careers."

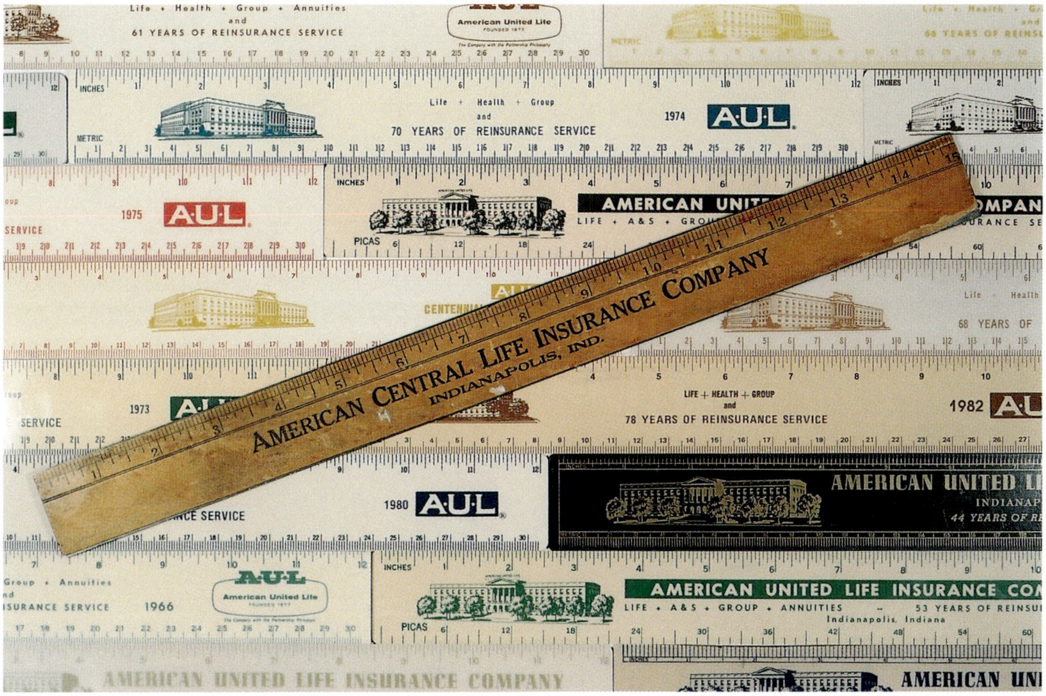

The so-called "reinsurance ruler" has been a popular promotional item of AUL's reinsurance operation since the days of American Central. A new plastic ruler is produced each year and, until 1999, that ruler had a complete calendar for the year on the back. Many AUL clients take pride in still possessing one of the oldest AUL reinsurance rulers.

It was the spring of 1977, but there still was plenty of snow in Aspen, Colorado, when this group attended an AUL executive workshop there. Former President Gerald Ford (front row, fifth from left) was a speaker at the workshop.

Clarence Jackson explains AUL's organization philosophy to Swedish life insurance agents Per-Erik Selander (left) and Lars-Erik Ohlsson, who visited the company in 1958 to see how AUL was preparing to use the National Cash Register 304 computer, which it had just ordered. The two men, who were with Thule Life Insurance Company of Stockholm, were brought to the United States for seven weeks by National Cash Register Company to survey computer equipment available in this country and how various companies planned to use it. According to long-time AUL employee Harold Thompson, because of the chart's shape and its frequent use by President Jackson, the organization chart became known around the company as the "football chart."

CHAPTER 12

THE COMPUTER AGE

The computer age at AUL really began on May 1, 1960. That is the day the NCR 304 was pronounced fully installed and ready for use.

The million-dollar computer took up 1,980 square feet of space—about the size of an average house—and special air-conditioning and humidity control equipment required an additional 600 square feet. A vapor-proof masonry wall surrounded the computer room, which also had a raised floor and special lighting. The computer, enclosed in glass walls so that it could be viewed by visitors to the building, could take input from both paper tape and punch cards, and it stored data on reels of magnetic tape.

AUL was the first insurance company to get an NCR 304, which was built by the National Cash Register Company and was at the time the state-of-the-art, transistorized electronic data processing system. Some competitors of NCR may have had similar computers, according to Tom Linzer, but "they didn't have all the bells and whistles of the 304." Linzer, a National Cash Register employee at the time, supervised the installation of the 304 at AUL.

In 1958, shortly after ordering the 304, AUL bought a much-smaller Remington Rand Univac 120. It used only punch cards, but it could be programmed to perform various functions and could be considered AUL's first computer. Ken Sneed, who began working in the company's tabulating department in 1950 and later was one of the first operators of the 304, said AUL had a programmable collator even before the Univac 120. And United Mutual and American Central had both been big users of punch cards long before their merger. But it was the NCR 304 that really began to change the way business was done at AUL and turned the tabulating department into the data processing department.

When the company ordered the NCR 304 in January 1958, only the first engineering model even existed. "AUL bought it on faith," Linzer said, and, as a result, it got one of the first units built, "maybe number five or six."

Linzer was working for the National Cash Register Company as a service technician, repairing typewriters and other office equipment, when in 1958 he was selected for training as a computer technician. The NCR 304 was developed at NCR's facility in Hawthorne, California, but General Electric Company built the major components at its factory in Phoenix, Arizona. So, in 1959, Linzer moved to Phoenix, where he was trained on the 304 and helped de-bug the system before the first units were shipped. When the U.S. Marine Corps got the first three units, Linzer helped install them. Then, in April 1960, he came to Indianapolis to serve as site manager for the installation of the 304 at AUL. Myron T. Fouke was the coordinator for AUL.

For the next four years, Linzer remained in Indianapolis, working for National Cash Register. By 1964 he had learned to program the computer and was looking for a new job. AUL hired him. "AUL's NCR 304 was performing well," he said, "but there is no question I was hired as an insurance policy." After twenty years with NCR, Linzer worked another twenty years for AUL, retiring in 1984 as manager of systems and programming, general. He said there were about ten people working in data processing when he arrived, more than a hundred when he retired.

One of those computer pioneers at AUL was Ken Sneed, who operated the 304 for a time and later was assistant manager of it. Another was Dolores Smith, who was hired in March 1960 to learn how to prepare input for the 304 and then to train others to do it.

Smith said a lot of employees were very apprehensive when the big computer was first put in service. "When the computer was first used to do calculations," she said, "the people who had been doing those by hand continued to do them manually because they didn't trust the computer. And a lot of people were afraid the computer was going to take their job." She also said the company liked to show off the computer, so there were frequent visitors to the computer room. "The guys started wearing coats and ties since they were never sure when Mr. Jackson might bring in a visitor," she said. Smith became a computer operator and later a programmer. She retired in 1998 after thirty-eight years with AUL. Sneed retired in 1986 after almost thirty-six years with the company.

At first, the NCR 304 was used to automate billing data and name-and-address files, but eventually it was programmed to handle most of the company's direct, reinsurance and accounting functions. Most policy records, however, were still being kept on punch cards in several different areas of the home office.

In 1969 the company supplemented the 304 with a leased IBM 360 Model 40, another mainframe computer. With it, IBM gave AUL the Advanced Life Insurance System (ALIS) software, which the company began immediately to adapt. To prepare for the IBM computer and ALIS, AUL in 1968 had appointed Edgar W. Pattison, the company's chief actuary, as director of data processing systems and programming. And despite some trauma—those involved might say "a lot of trauma"—the switch to IBM resulted eventually in greatly increased accuracy and efficiency. "ALIS was a significant advance," Linzer said.

AUL had found that many insurance companies were working together to develop programs that ran on IBM computers. Using the NCR 304, AUL had

There was nothing "personal" about this computer! Several men were required to move the central processing unit of the NCR 304 into the AUL building in April 1960. Tom Linzer (right) supervised the operation.

By May 1, 1960, the NCR 304 was up and running.

Tom Linzer (far right), who was then the AUL site manager for National Cash Register Company, demonstrates the NCR 304's high-speed card reader for (from left) L. S. Norman, J. Howard Alltop, Edward M. Karrmann, and Clarence A. Jackson.

to do everything for itself without enough people to do it effectively. L. S. Norman, senior vice president at that time, said, "We finally realized we had to give up what we were trying to do and go with the other (insurance) companies." And AUL did not just switch to IBM. In 1969 it also combined with fourteen other insurance companies to form a corporation called Insurance Systems of America, which was to design and sell general life programs for insurance company systems. AUL later purchased several programs from ISA.

The venerable NCR 304 was finally retired in 1976 and sold for $4,000 to American Greeting Card Company, which wanted it for spare parts. At the time, the Smithsonian Institution expressed an interest in acquiring the 304 for its historical value, but nothing came of that.

The IBM 360/40 used new disk drives that were faster than the NCR 304 and had a larger capacity to store more information in less space, but by the 1970s the technology was advancing rapidly. In 1972, AUL acquired a more advanced computer, the IBM 370/145, and in 1973 it got still newer disk drives. Not long after came the IBM 370/158, then the IBM 3032 and then the IBM 3033-N. The 3032, which went into operation at AUL in March 1980, had a "memory" of four million positions, or bytes. The 370/158 had had a memory of two million bytes. The 360/40, from a decade earlier, had a memory of 196,000 bytes. The NCR 304, from two decades back, had a memory of 48,000 bytes. And when AUL installed the 3033-N in March 1981, it was 40 percent faster than the mainframe installed just a year earlier.

Even before the arrival of the IBM computer, data-processing staff hours were often extended. After the arrival of the 360/40, the department went to two shifts a day, then three shifts a day Monday through Friday. Over the years, that schedule continued to grow. In 2001, the computer was operating twenty-four hours a day six days a week and twelve hours on Sunday.

During the 1970s AUL added a system for yearly renewable term insurance, a system for tax-deferred annuities, a credit life system, a payroll system, plus systems to handle the general ledger, automatic bank checks, stock and bond accounting, and mortgage loan accounting. Other systems included the Alpha Index, a check-writing system, and a repetitive payments system. Some of these systems were purchased, others written by AUL's electronic data processing personnel.

With the new computers and the new systems came CRT (cathode ray tube) units, or terminals. There were two CRT terminals in the home office in 1975, thirty by 1979. By that time, there were also two CRTs in the field offices, the beginning of an agency computer network.

In August 1971 Ed Pattison, now vice president for electronic data processing, hired Keith Bennett as a systems analyst. Bennett had gained data processing experience and management experience at two other life insurance companies, and in 1973 he was named director of electronic data processing, reporting to Pattison, who remained as chief actuary. In 1975, Bennett was promoted to vice president.

"We kept getting larger computers as we added more applications," Bennett said, "and we had formed a committee called the EDP Management Committee. All new systems and new hardware had to be approved by the EDP Management Committee. . . . We didn't want technology for technology's sake. We wanted to use technology to meet the business need, and that committee helped us do that. We also had a primary systems coordinator for each product division."

The pension and group departments both developed major systems in the mid-seventies, Bennett said. Then, in the late seventies or early eighties, he said, "we gave the field force access to the ALIS records through terminals in the agency offices. That was a relatively significant decision for the individual division to allow agents to access directly the home-office records. Instead of writing in or phoning in, they could access those records directly. They could also do sales illustrations."

About the same time, the company began using mini-computers, most of them Wang computers. The company's centralized word-processing center used a Wang. Others were used for calculations by the actuaries. "Two things caused the Wangs to be done away with," Bennett said. "IBM came out with something called the Displaywriter, which was an individual word-processing

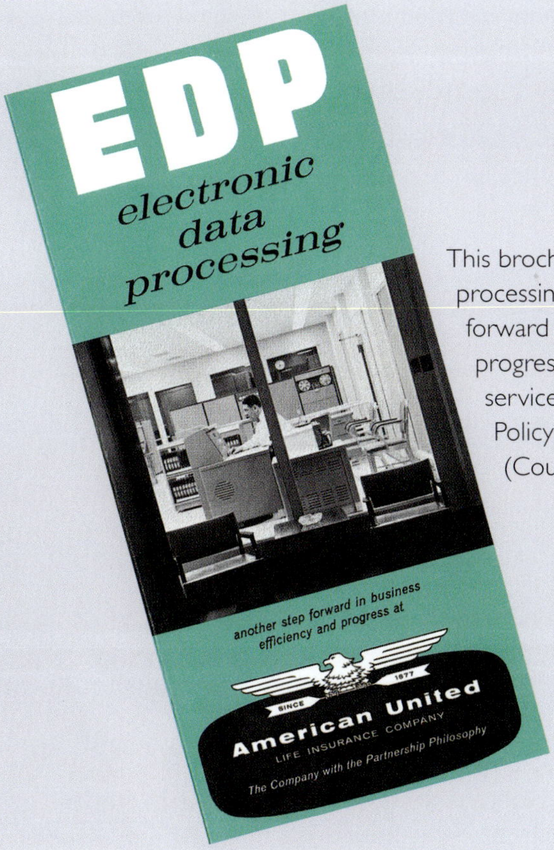

This brochure touts electronic data processing—EDP—as "another step forward in business efficiency and progress," thus providing "better service to American United Policyholders and Agents." (Courtesy Dolores Smith)

machine, and they gave decentralized control to the user of word processing. Then came personal computers. The actuaries were the first to get PCs because they had a lot of calculating power—as much as or more than the Wangs—and this was further decentralization of computing power into the hands of the actual user."

AUL acquired its first personal computer in 1983 (64K memory, floppy disks, cost $4,544). "A major influence on us there," Bennett said, "was the fact that IBM had gotten into the personal computer business. It sort of legitimized the personal computer."

In the mid-1980s the department's name was changed from Electronic Data Processing (EDP) to Information Systems (IS), and with that change came a lot of other changes. The pension division purchased a new system called MAAS that ran on a Hewlett-Packard computer, the company's first HP. The pension IS staff then moved into the pension division, the beginning of the decentralization of IS staff. Also, the company began replacing typewriters with IBM personal typing system (PTS) units, which were personal computers with a typewriter-like keyboard and printer. Then came HP LaserJet printers, more modern PCs, and an internal electronic mail and calendaring system called EMS (electronic mail system). With EMS, it was possible to send messages throughout the company electronically, instead of sending a memo, and it was now possible to check a person's calendar and schedule a meeting on line as well.

In 1990 AUL invested in its first local area network (LAN) to see what it could do. Two years later, it installed fiber optic cable throughout the building and began networking computers into LANs. Through the LANs, PCs were connected to each other and to the mainframe. This was a fundamental

Keith Bennett joined AUL in 1971, and became director of electronic data processing in 1973. He headed AUL's computer operations until the end of 1994, when he retired as senior vice president for systems.

change, because it gave people throughout the company access to the same data and allowed the sharing of devices such as printers.

In 1991 AUL got another in what by now was a long string of new mainframe computers, the IBM 9121-440. But by this time, the mainframe was just a part of a multifaceted technology system. There was even talk about doing away with the mainframe computer. "The conventional thinking—and not just in the insurance industry," Bennett said, "was that PCs were getting bigger and more powerful and they were being networked. The significant thing that brought about the idea that the mainframe could be discontinued was the networking of the PCs—and also using servers, which are large PCs. You hook the personal computers to the servers and you have, in effect, the computing power to replace the IBM mainframe. That happened, but it didn't replace the mainframe. In fact, some of the networking was done through the mainframe, and the servers talked to the mainframe too."

Keith Bennett retired at the end of 1994. He was succeeded by Scott Kincaid, who was given the title of vice president and chief information officer. Kincaid had been with AUL since 1985 and had helped develop the company's first disaster recovery plan, now considered a necessity for any company in the types of business AUL is in. "It's very consistent with AUL's fundamental principle of providing peace of mind to our policyowners," he said. "Right now, if you lose the AUL Tower, which is a rather daunting thought, AUL should be able to survive fine."

A major change in the way technology was used at AUL began to occur in 1994 when the company entered into a strategic alliance with The State Life Insurance Company of Indianapolis. The two companies were linked, but State Life was going to remain in its own building and continue to market its

Administrative secretary Virginia House went on vacation in the spring of 1988 and when she returned she found her typewriter had been replaced by this personal typing system. "I cussed it the first week I had it," she said later, "but now I don't think I could live without it." The PTS was a scaled-down version of the IBM PS2/30 computer, reduced in size to better fit a secretarial desk, and came with its own dedicated word processing software. It could also be used as a correcting typewriter when paired with the IBM Correcting Quietwriter printer. AUL purchased 31 of the PTS units in November 1987.

own products. A similar arrangement followed with Pioneer Mutual Life Insurance Company, of Fargo, North Dakota. CNL Financial Corporation, of Macon, Georgia, was acquired and AUL International was established in Coral Gables, Florida. At the same time, some of AUL's home office staff moved into other nearby buildings—the Julian Building and the Capital Center. Technology played a key role in pulling everything together, but the networking had become a lot more complicated.

"Those are now all connected," Kincaid said, "you can sign on to the LAN at most of those locations. I think State Life was the beginning of a series of events that changed the shape of AUL. Forget the technology. We are not as Tower-focused anymore. We're more a conglomerate."

Then came the Internet, which gave AUL additional links to the outside world. In 1996 AUL established its own web site at **www.aul.com**. Developed basically as an electronic brochure through corporate communications, the web site served as a public relations tool, increasing awareness of AUL. "That was just brochureware, a little basic advertising of who AUL is," Kincaid said. "Netserve (1998) is where we actually let people [using the Internet] go in and inquire about their 401(k) funds and make changes in their contributions. We also connected EMS to the Internet and, we take it for granted now, but we could for the first time send e-mail anywhere."

Kincaid said the largest technology project AUL ever undertook—by far—was getting all of AUL's technology ready for Year 2000. "Most of the systems, unfortunately, were very date sensitive and would not work properly after 1999," he said. "Insurance processing by its nature is date sensitive." Work on Y2K began in 1996. Kevin Weston was appointed Y2K program director and spearheaded AUL's efforts from the outset.

Zenith laptop computers similar to this one and portable Diconix printers began showing up in the offices of AUL agents across the country in the summer of 1988. At that time, new software with a point-of-sale version of AUL's Financial Need Analysis was introduced that would let agents use the laptops to make presentations "live" in clients' homes and offices.

"The goal was to go into '99 knowing that most of the systems were ready," Kincaid said.

The people at AUL did such a good job they wound up creating and hosting a Y2K user group that aided a number of other companies, but, as they approached Year 2000, they were still leaving nothing to chance. They set up an event management center about a week before New Year's Day, 2000, and they were prepared for any eventuality.

"The good news is that, with the many system changes, things worked great and our contingency plans didn't have to be used," Kincaid said. "The other good news is it was the best year-end ever, and we learned a lot. We got statements out the fastest, had fewer errors, and got the ledger closed quicker than ever before. Our goal was to make sure that, on the first work day, everything was fine for our customers."

According to Weston, about five hundred people at AUL worked on some aspect of Y2K, almost one hundred worked some time over the New Year's weekend, and, over four years, almost two hundred person years of work went into the project. The total cost, he said, was $18.1 million.

As technology continues to play a major role in the insurance industry, maintaining a balance between cutting-edge systems and controlling costs on behalf of AUL's policyholders is vital. In 2001, AUL introduced a new chief information officer, Steven Weber, who replaced Kincaid. Weber brings a unique and refreshing perspective to the systems side of the business.

"My primary task is to make certain we directly support what our business divisions want to accomplish," said Weber. "We need to address technology in a very strategic manner. We have to make certain we do the right thing at the right time and in the right way."

Steven Weber became senior vice president of systems and chief information officer of AUL in 2001. Steve made an immediate and major impact on a revised business continuation plan, Retirement Services Omni System implementation and other systems projects and processes vital to the support of AUL and its partner companies.

In 2001 the systems department—the name was changed from information systems in 1993—still had an IBM mainframe computer and the ALIS system, acquired in 1969, was still working. But the IBM 3000-H50 has a memory of two billion bytes, compared with 48,000 for the NCR 304 and 196,000 for the first IBM mainframe AUL got. AUL, in 2001, also had a number of other large computers and an inventory of 2,500 personal computers—more PCs than people—and most of those computers were connected to the world via the Internet.

At five minutes after midnight on New Year's Day 2000, staffers toasted—non-alcoholic, of course—the New Year and, more important, the success of AUL's Y2K project. Celebrating that night were (from left) Kevin Weston, Linda Elrod, Cindy Duran, Carol Weaver, Dave Marks, Scott Kincaid, and Kathrine Starnes.

Team leaders on the Y2K project included (from left, front row) Donna Hearne, Pam Becker, Bonita Kline, Carol Weaver, Mike Taylor, Bill Jackson; (middle row) Barbara Martin, Terry Nicodemus, Cindy Duran, Scott Kincaid, Jerry Fromholz, Kevin Weston; (back row) Jerry Minth, Schuyler Schmidt, Michael Barnett, Felicia Maclin, Kristi Abbott, and Jon Fulk.

CHAPTER 13

RETIREMENT SERVICES — A GROWTH INDUSTRY

Not long after the merger of United Mutual and American Central, the company began developing a group annuity, and it sold its first group annuity in 1938. The contract covered 109 persons and brought in $1,505. In 1939 AUL sold three more group annuity policies, bringing in $1,488. The company was in the pension business.

During the 1940s and early '50s, the pension business was slow. There were some years when AUL did not sell a single group annuity. Business picked up somewhat after President Clarence Jackson created a group department in 1955 and began promoting group products, including pension products. But then a combination of events thrust AUL into the pension business in a big way.

In 1958 Congress passed what became known as 403(b) legislation, allowing employees of hospitals, public schools and certain other nonprofit organizations to invest in tax-deferred annuities. Group Vice President Sherman Jenson and Group Actuary Richard Miller began pushing AUL to get serious about the pension business, and the company hired George Reiger and Leland Schmitt away from Bankers Life of Iowa, where they had been involved in pension marketing. Then Hamilton Gardner and William White, who in 1963 formed an Indianapolis-based organization to market employee benefits, approached AUL about developing a group tax-deferred annuity product that their company could sell to hospitals and schools.

Schmitt, who became senior vice president and secretary of Fidelity Security Life Insurance Company in Kansas City (he died in October 2001), said AUL hired Reiger to head its pension operation in 1961. He joined Reiger in 1963. And they liked Gardner and White's proposal.

Gardner and White had been turned down by one or more other companies before they got to AUL, according to Schmitt. "There weren't many people who were interested," he said. "They thought hospital employees didn't make much money, and it [the market] was small potatoes for them." But when AUL agreed to develop the product, that decision began a relationship that continues today and a relationship that over the years has produced an enormous amount of business for both AUL and Gardner and White, Inc.

David Schweitzer, now a vice president at Gardner and White, worked at AUL in the late 1960s. One of his jobs then was to coordinate AUL's business with Gardner and White. He said AUL designed several products primarily for Gardner and White and worked hard getting those products approved in states where Gardner and White developed markets. And that effort paid off.

John Lauter, who began work at AUL in 1954 and worked in pension administration for many years, said, "AUL was one of the first—if not *the* first—to offer a group product for the tax-sheltered annuity line. Up to that time, some insurance companies had been selling individual policies, endowment type policies or annuities to the tax-sheltered market, but these were not really good products for the teachers and other not-for-profits because they had very high withdrawal charges. . . . So, when we moved into this product line and offered this, we could pretty much have our choice of customers because we were so far ahead of the insurance industry."

In 1969 AUL developed a group variable annuity, and in the early 1970s it developed its first computer system for the administration of pension products. Competition in the pension business increased considerably in the 1970s, but Congress also created a big, new market by passing legislation in 1974 authorizing individual retirement accounts (IRAs).

By this time, AUL had its own regional sales offices selling group and pension products, and it had marketing agreements with other brokerage firms, such as Zahorik Company in Pasadena, California, and Dow Laney Corporation, in Seattle, Washington. Gardner and White, however, was still

John Lauter worked at AUL for thirty-nine years, retiring in 1993 as vice president for annuity services. He served as personnel director for about ten years before joining the pension department in the early 1970s.

AUL's biggest producer—so big, in fact, that AUL became so concerned about the large concentration of business from one source that in 1977 it stopped taking new tax-deferred annuity business from Gardner and White for a time. Fortunately, that moratorium was later dropped, and today Gardner and White is still a major marketer of AUL pension products.

Richard F. Aller, who had worked for Bankers Life of Iowa, was hired in 1977 to head the group department and strengthen and streamline both the group insurance and pension operations. Both lines continued to grow rapidly, and in 1982 Chairman Jack Reich split the department. Aller continued to head the group operations. James P. Shanahan was hired to manage pension operations. He had been head of the pension division at Union Central Life Insurance Company in Cincinnati.

After forming the new pension department, which officially began operating January 1, 1983, Shanahan began working to improve service and to develop some new products. One of those products was designed to accommodate the new 401(k) plans, created by Congress in 1980. He also went looking for a new computer system. "We had an antiquated computerized system," he said, "which did not do the entire package of administration electronically. A lot of work had to be done manually. Also, we couldn't offer multi-fund products." On July 1, 1985, the company signed a contract with Financial Data Products (FDP) of Coral Gables, Florida, to provide AUL with

James Shanahan (right), head of AUL's pension operations from 1982 until his retirement in 1997, reviews figures with K. B. Wilson in 1989. At that time, Wilson was managing partner of the Gardner and White employee benefit consulting firm, AUL's leading producer of group annuity premium for many years. Wilson worked at AUL from 1957 to 1974, serving as the company's general counsel and corporate secretary from 1970 to 1974. At Gardner and White, he became managing partner in 1977 and later president when the company was incorporated. He retired in 1994.

a sophisticated computer system called MAAS (Multiple Account Annuity System).

Staffers from AUL's information systems division began installing MAAS, but with the pension division also involved, Shanahan said, "it was a two-headed monster." Maybe that was because MAAS ran on a Hewlett-Packard computer, the first at AUL. In any event, Shanahan said, "We brought in the consulting arm of Coopers and Lybrand, and they recommended that we decentralize, transfer everything over to the pension division. So, at that time, we transferred a number of people from centralized IS to the pension division, and things went much smoother after that."

That first decentralization of technical staffers happened around the same time a much larger reorganization occurred at AUL that resulted in the creation of four completely separate product divisions: individual, group, pensions, and reinsurance. The senior officer in each division was given bottom-line responsibility, along with authority over all aspects of product development, marketing, and administration.

It took about five years to complete the implementation of MAAS. "The first thing we had to do was install the base system," Shanahan said. "Our number-two priority was to get one or two new products up and running—one for Gardner and White and one that we could market to qualified plans. Then we began to fine-tune the installation of it [MAAS], and the real challenge was to convert the contracts that we had over to it. . . . Because we converted contracts on their anniversary dates, it took three or four years. We didn't have the capacity to do it all at once."

With MAAS in full service, the pension division was able in 1993 to begin adding outside mutual funds as investment options. The first funds were from Fidelity Investments. "That was a coup for us to even get Fidelity because other companies that had asked about it had been turned down," Shanahan said. "They liked the quality of our operation, what they saw and the possibilities they saw. . . . And when we put in the funds, our sales took off and never looked back."

Shanahan said the company reached $1 billion in pension reserves in 1982, the year he joined the company. By 1995 it had passed $4 billion. Pension assets increased an average of $232 million a year during his tenure with the company, with an average annual after-tax gain of $17.5 million. There were about fifty employees in the pension area in 1982, Shanahan said, and more than five hundred when he retired in 1997.

William L. Tindall replaced Shanahan in August 1997, coming from Massachusetts Mutual Life Insurance Company, where he had worked for more than twenty-five years. What he found was a market where AUL's competition had increased. "I think up until maybe 1996 or '97 we were below the radar screen of a lot of our competitors," he said. "With the success of the mid-nineties in the 401(k) area, we became known to our competitors and they were a little bit better able to compete with us."

He also found a maturing market, where plan sponsors were more sophisticated, and a market where the Internet was beginning to have a big impact. In 1998 the pension division began a study to determine the division's systems need in the twenty-first century. That study led to what Tindall called "a complete re-build of our infrastructure."

"We are replacing the record-keeping system and voice response system," he said, "rebuilding the Internet, putting in new commission and reserve systems, and building new linkages to the investment providers that we deal with, such as Fidelity, American Century and Invesco. And we are re-engineering our work flows as well. This is roughly a $24 million project that really is aimed at helping us achieve operational excellence."

One key, Tindall noted, is service support for clients. The division, now known as Retirement Services, has thirty-six sales representatives in twenty-two offices around the country, and it has twenty-six service representatives. "The service reps," he said, "help the sales reps by dealing with the great detail that's involved when we set up a new piece of business and in providing continuing support that supplements what we do here in the home office. It frees up the sales reps to do more selling."

To continue to grow in the retirement services field, according to Tindall, AUL must provide consistently good service, cut unit costs, and earn a reputation as a customer-friendly organization. He believes technology will be "both the enabler and the driver." And after extensive study, the division is installing a new record-keeping system called Omni Plus, developed by Sungard Corporation.

"We picked Omni because they are the industry leader," Tindall said. "They are by far the biggest in the record-keeping system area." His division is

William L. Tindall joined AUL in 1997 as senior vice president for the pension division, succeeding James Shanahan. The name of the division was later changed to retirement services division.

moving into an electronic environment where it can receive contributions and contribution data electronically as well as process benefits electronically.

"The Internet is becoming critical for us," Tindall remarked. "If a person wants a loan, he or she can go on line and process it and we can probably get a check in the mail in twenty-four hours, whereas if it were paper, it might take two weeks. We can process it on the Internet for pennies. And part of the whole strategy is, if you can do it electronically, you can do it faster, you can reduce errors, you can provide more functionality, and more and more today, as people are hooked up to the Internet, they want this additional choice."

Today Retirement Services is generating a significant portion of AUL's profit each year, and it has been growing its premium at a compound annual growth rate of 14 percent over the last five years. In 2001, contributions from new and existing clients were a record-high $974 million, almost the amount of total pension assets in 1982. The division staff is also growing, with about 650 people in the home office and the field.

AUL's success in the retirement services business has come from defined contribution plans, such as the 401(k) and 403(b) products, and Gardner and White is still an important part of that success.

"We wouldn't be where we are today without the support of Gardner and White," Tindall said. "In fact, today they have about $1.5 billion in assets with us, so they are still a very important part of our success.

"We are very fortunate. A really good foundation was built by the people who preceded me and allowed us to get to this point. The growth has slowed a little bit in the retirement plan area, but they (experts) are still expecting double-digit growth over the next five to ten years. And we think, if we do what we know we need to do, we are going to play an ever-bigger role in the future.

"Our vision today is to become *the* premier customer-focused organization specializing in the small retirement plan market. . . . I would say we are already in the top ten."

CHAPTER 14

THE DISTRIBUTION SYSTEM

When the Knights of Pythias created its insurance program, lodge officers sold the insurance and collected the premiums, but eventually the lodge recognized the value of having trained agents help sell the life insurance.

One of those early agents was Guss R. Merritt, who was living in Monticello, Indiana, in 1923, selling shoes for a living, when Harry Wade, president of the Knights of Pythias Insurance Department, hired him to call on lodge members and sell them life insurance. Merritt traveled all over northern Indiana, first by train, later by car. His son-in-law, Bob Brady, said Guss would leave home on Monday morning and return on Friday night. He would call on lodge members in their homes as well as at lodge meetings. He received a dollar for each thousand dollars of life insurance he sold.

Merritt became one of the Knights of Pythias' top agents, Brady said, and for a time Wade paid him a salary, not just commissions, to keep from losing him. In 1932, after the lodge established United Mutual Life Insurance Company to replace its Insurance Department, Wade encouraged Merritt to move to Lafayette, where he would have easier access to more people. With United Mutual, agents were no longer limited to selling to lodge members only.

For many years, Merritt collected the premiums on insurance he sold, which gave him regular access to people all over northern Indiana and gave him

Guss R. Merritt began selling life insurance for the Knights of Pythias Insurance Department in 1923. He later sold for United Mutual and then AUL, retiring in 1952.

more opportunities to sell insurance. "And what Guss wrote stayed on the books," said Brady, who in recent years has serviced some of those policyholders.

After the merger of United Mutual and American Central Life Insurance Company in 1937, Guss became an agent for the new company, American United Life Insurance Company, and his agent contract was changed, eliminating some of the benefits he enjoyed before. What Merritt resented the most, however, Brady said, was that agents from American Central were allowed to keep their old contracts and receive benefits others didn't. He attributed the policy to the fact that former American Central executives had most of the positions of power at AUL. At the time of the merger, American Central also had a larger and more established field force that United Mutual.

Bob Brady became an agent for AUL in 1946 and joined his father-in-law in the Lafayette agency. He became the agency manager in 1952 when health problems forced Merritt to retire, and in 2002 Brady was still representing AUL in the Lafayette area. Brady is a member of the Million Dollar Round Table and the AUL President's Club.

"When I started with AUL," Brady said, "we sold lots of twenty-pay endowments at age sixty-five. That was the best product." Then the company began to improve the other products, he said, and he began to sell more ordinary life.

AUL's field force suffered from neglect for a number of years following the merger. Apparently because of the conflict between executives who came from United Mutual and those who came from American Central, there was little leadership and almost no effort to recruit or train new agents. There were agencies, but no real agency system. This was the situation that faced Eber M.

Robert "Bob" Brady, son-in-law of Guss Merritt, went to work for Guss at his Lafayette, Indiana, agency in 1946. He took over the agency when Merritt retired and he was still representing AUL in the Lafayette area in 2002. This picture was taken in 1984.

Spence, CLU, when he was hired as vice president and director of agencies in 1948 by the new president, Leslie Crouch.

"Ebe" Spence, as he was known, was a college graduate with years of experience as an insurance agent and general agent, most recently with the Indianapolis agency of Provident Mutual Life Insurance Company. He was widely respected in the industry, and, a year after he was hired, he was elected to the company's board of directors.

When he was hired, Spence set out immediately to build a professional field force. He set up protected territories for agencies, and he began to recruit and train people. "He didn't put anyone in those jobs who hadn't carried a rate book (sold insurance)," said Max Hittle, CLU, a Northwestern Mutual agent when Spence recruited him to serve as a superintendent of agencies. Robert Thompson was hired to fill a full-time position as training director.

Many of the persons Spence attracted to AUL had distinguished careers with the company. Some went on to earn even more recognition elsewhere. Frank Sullivan, CLU, AUL's agency manager in South Bend for a number of years, was at age forty-two the youngest person ever elected president of the Million Dollar Round Table. He was later president of Mutual Benefit Life Insurance Company. Eugene M. Busche was recruited in 1950 right out of Indiana University. He worked three years as an agent under Guss Merritt in Lafayette and then was brought into the home office as an agency assistant. He later went to Indianapolis Life Insurance Company, where he eventually rose to the position of chairman, president, and chief executive officer.

James Comstock, CLU, was hired in 1953 and opened an Indianapolis agency in the Circle Tower downtown. American Central had established an Indianapolis agency in 1931 but it was closed in 1952 when the agency man-

Eber "Ebe" Spence, CLU, was hired as AUL's vice president and director of agencies in 1948, and he immediately set out to build a knowledgeable and professional field force. He only held the position for ten years, but he had a great impact on AUL's agency system. Spence served on AUL's board of directors from 1948 to 1968.

ager, Morris Conn, suffered a heart attack and took a job in the home office. The agency had been staffed by part-time agents. Comstock began hiring full-time, career agents, and many of the people he recruited during a thirty-year career with AUL are still with the company in 2002, including Jerry Semler.

Clarence Jackson replaced Leslie Crouch as president in 1952, and Jackson and Ebe Spence had serious philosophical differences. Spence was strictly a life-insurance man. Jackson was a businessman who had been hired to run an insurance company. Their differences led to Spence's retirement in 1958.

Spence remained on AUL's board until 1968, but he was replaced as vice president and director of agencies by Lawrence "Pete" Leland, whom he had recruited a decade earlier as assistant director of agencies. Leland continued to build the AUL field force with emphasis on quality, but he later left for a top position with National Life Insurance Company of Vermont.

Spence was director of agencies for only ten years, but he remained active on a consulting basis for the company. During his ten years as agency leader, AUL's individual insurance business increased 250 percent. In 1937, the first year after the merger, AUL had new life insurance sales of $20.8 million. New life sales were only $26 million in 1948, when Spence was hired. By 1958 they were $88 million and going up every year. Spence was a founder of the Life Insurance Marketing Institute at Purdue University and a leader at the local, state and national level in the Association of Life Underwriters, as well as other insurance organizations. And he left a lasting impression on the AUL field force.

Spence, a great believer in performance, created AUL's system where agency heads are called general agents, not agency managers, and are compensated on the basis of production, not paid a flat salary. He also believed in education and encouraged agents to earn the Chartered Life Underwriter (CLU) designation. James Comstock, who came to AUL from Indianapolis Life, was the only CLU in the AUL field force in 1953. By 1966 the company had enough agents who, through study and training, had earned the CLU designation that it ranked among the top 3 percent of the nation's insurance companies in this important measure of professionalism. In addition, in 1966 AUL had a record 112 career agents receive the National Quality Award, given by the National Association of Life Underwriters for sales and service to clients.

American Central and AUL had always sold their reinsurance services through special sales representatives, not through agents. In 1955 Clarence Jackson created a group department to offer a full line of group life insurance and annuities, and soon special sales offices were established around the country to sell these products. AUL agents were encouraged to sell the group products, but most had little interest. Some doubted their salability. At that point, however, AUL had three channels of distribution. A few years later, when the company became a major producer and marketer of pension products, an additional distribution system was developed.

For most AUL agents, however, the products they chose to sell were individual products and the system, at least for newer agents, was quite structured. Morris "Moe" Silverman, CLU, of Indianapolis, still a top agent for AUL, recalled:

"When I started in the business in 1959, I had to learn the Shielder. It was a whole sales presentation built around a life-paid-up-at-seventy contract. A neat product, and we literally had to memorize a sales presentation. I had an answer to any objection you could possibly throw at me. Also, we had a cookie jar: 'Who's going to keep the cookie jar full?' This was a pictured sales presentation and closing. I think we had eighteen closes—literally eighteen closes—and, I don't care what you were going to do, you were going to get all eighteen."

Silverman said at first sales were slow in coming despite the prepared sales presentation. "I'm sure I looked at the want ads at least once a week those first couple of years," he said. "It's a tough business. You've got to deal with rejection." But Silverman stuck with it. He qualified for AUL's Leaders Club the first time he was eligible. He just missed qualifying for the higher-level President's Club the next time, and he has been a President's Club qualifier ever since. Silverman has also been a member of AUL's Chairman's Council, composed of the company's top twelve agents, longer than anyone else.

He said good work habits and an ability to deal with rejection are essential

In 1974, the marketing department began recognizing its sales leaders each month on this display board in the department.

John M. Cantu, CLU, displayed AUL's 1978 sales campaign in this photo taken for the *AULnews*. Cantu joined AUL in 1970 and became vice president for marketing in 1973. He was named senior vice president for marketing in 1975 and served in that position until 1981, when he left to become president of Federal Home Life Insurance Company.

if a person is going to succeed as a life insurance agent. "Early on, I kept records," he said. "I used to stay down at the office on Monday. Judi [his wife] knew I wouldn't be home for dinner. I would make phone calls, and I kept track. If I made seventeen phone calls, I got one appointment. If I got five appointments, I got one sale. And that's a lot of no's."

Silverman doesn't use a memorized spiel anymore, but he said for him at least the selling of life insurance has not changed much during his forty-two-plus years with AUL. "My interviews are still held with a yellow legal pad, or maybe a white one," he said. "We sit and talk and we deal with faith, trust, and confidence." But he acknowledges that much about the business has changed, including the products being sold, the competition, and the technology involved in selling and servicing AUL's clients.

Under Clarence Jackson, AUL began offering health and accident insurance and a full line of group life insurance and annuities. The company also expanded its activity in the reinsurance area. "We've got a department store of insurance," Jackson would say. "We used to sell only to individuals, but now we sell to business firms and partnerships." By the 1960s, AUL was selling a lot of group life insurance, group annuities and accident and health insurance, as well as individual life and life reinsurance.

By the 1970s the computer began to have an impact on the field force. Wayne O. McHargue, ChFC, CLU, CFP, of Indianapolis, was one of the first AUL agents to make insurance calls carrying two briefcases—one containing a computer terminal. He would begin an interview with a client by gathering

AUL chairman Jerry Semler (left) presents Morris "Moe" Silverman, CLU, an award for being AUL's top agent for the eighteen-month contest period ending in 1996, the second time he had been the top agent, based on first-year commissions. Silverman has qualified for the company's Chairman's Council, composed of the top twelve agents, twenty-five times—more than any other agent.

data on his or her needs and objectives. Then he would open his briefcase computer terminal next to a telephone and dial a toll-free number that connected him with Computone's computer in Atlanta, Georgia. He would feed the data about his client into the computer in Atlanta, and almost immediately a voice, through a computer terminal, would begin reeling off answers to questions about the client's insurance needs, tax liabilities, and the like. With the computer terminal, McHargue said, he could spend less time with a client and accomplish more.

Within a few years, AUL had linked all of its agencies and regional sales offices with the home office through a system of IBM personal computers and special leased-line telephone service. This Direct Access Remote Terminal (DART) system made possible quick, accurate communications and faster service, eliminating the need for the services offered by Computone.

The computer also made possible enormous changes in the products themselves, and in 1983 AUL introduced American Universal Life, an interest-sensitive product that combined protection with the higher yield of an investment vehicle. AUL had been a pioneer in the marketing of group tax-deferred annuities and other pension products and, with the coming of the computer age, that business mushroomed. Congress gave it a boost in 1974 with legislation authorizing individual retirement accounts (IRAs) and another boost in 1980 with a bill creating 401(k) defined-contribution plans. By the mid-eighties, AUL had a computer system that would allow it to offer products with multiple investment options.

In 1987 AUL created four separate product divisions—individual, group, pensions (now called retirement services), and reinsurance. Each division sought to strengthen its own distribution system.

In 1976, Wayne O. McHargue, ChFC, CLU, CFP, of Indianapolis, was one of the first AUL agents to make insurance calls carrying two briefcases, one containing a KeyPact computer terminal. From his terminal, McHargue could dial a toll-free number that connected him with Computone's computer in Atlanta, where he could feed in data and receive answers to questions about his client's insurance needs, tax liabilities, and the like.

That same year, Dayton Molendorp, CLU, joined the individual division. He came from Mutual Security Life Insurance Company in Fort Wayne, Indiana, a company that was folding. In 1987 AUL offered contracts to Mutual Security's agents and, with court approval, in 1992 it bought Mutual Security's individual business. With a certain amount of pride, Molendorp points out that four of AUL's top ten agencies today came from Mutual Security.

With computers came the product revolution of the 1980s that brought interest-sensitive products and more sophisticated variable products with multi-fund options. For AUL, with Mutual Security's people came an interest in individual annuities. "When the Mutual Security agents joined us," said Jerry Semler, "they came out of an environment of selling a lot of annuities. Even though the annuities paid a lower commission, they were getting a lot of volume, and their experience helped us get established in the individual fixed annuity business."

Molendorp helped make it happen. "That was the first product John Barbre [senior vice president of the individual division at the time] asked me to develop when I got here," Molendorp said. "We (AUL) were huge on the TDA [tax-deferred annuity] side in the pension area, but we had no individual single premium annuity business to speak of. Then we had years in 1988, '89 and '90 when we did as much as $85 million a year. The product was a hot one. . . . Today between fixed and variable annuities on the individual side, we've got about a billion dollars under management. And that's happened since '88."

Molendorp became head of the individual division at AUL in 1999 when John Barbre retired, and he said one of his biggest challenges is keeping up with the changes taking place in the business. He started selling life insurance in

John Barbre, CLU, succeeded John Cantu as vice president for marketing in 1981. He became senior vice president for the individual division in 1987 and retired in 1999, after twenty-seven years with the company.

1974 in rural Iowa as an agent for Mutual Security, where he too learned a sales talk, called "You'll Earn a Fortune."

"When I came into the business," he said, "probably 85 percent of the premium sold in the individual marketplace was ordinary life insurance and probably ten to 15 percent was term insurance. There were versions of those products, but those were the two products that were being sold. Now, come fast forward to 2002, and all the barriers are down. The banks are in our business. The wire houses [stockbrokers] are in our business. The insurance companies are in the business. The mutual fund companies are in the business. And you have to look hard to find someone who calls themselves a life insurance company. Even the Northwestern Mutual, kind of the bastion of par, whole life insurance is now the Northwestern Mutual Financial Network."

Molendorp said one big change for the life insurance companies has been the move to variable products, both accumulation annuity products and life insurance. "That's the growth engine of the business today," he said. Another big change has been the emphasis on financial planning, where the product at the point of sale might be life insurance, an annuity, a mutual fund, or a stock trade. "It's not a product push," he said. "It's a planning push."

AUL is part of the financial services industry today. Almost no one disputes that. Some agents, such as Moe Silverman, still sell few variable products and express concern about what Silverman called "this chinking away at trust, faith and confidence." But more and more customers seem to be seeking products with higher risk and potentially greater reward and products where they can manage the investments themselves. "I don't think peoples' needs have changed," Molendorp said. "I think their wants have changed. With the improvements in medicine and with the success of the stock market,

Dayton Molendorp, CLU, who came to AUL in 1987 from Mutual Security Life Insurance Company in Fort Wayne, has headed individual operations since John Barbre retired in 1999.

most people aren't worried about dying too soon. They're worried about living too long. They're worried about the quality of their retirement. Their need for premature death coverage hasn't gone away, but their focus is on themselves into the future."

Current laws have made it easy for banks, stockbrokers, and insurance companies all to serve this market, and sophisticated technology has made it possible to design and service sophisticated products. The cost of technology is high, however, and the profit margins are small. So, AUL is seeking growth in all of its product lines, and, through the mutual holding company structure, it is broadening its product line and its channels of distribution.

"State Life has a niche," Molendorp said. "It's called impaired-risk life insurance. The people at State Life reach out through a wide distribution channel of brokers, and they use underwriting expertise to take cases that other mainline insurers have either declined or highly rated. They build product and pricing and match it up with seasoned impaired-risk underwriting to meet a need in the marketplace. We can then take that line back to the career agency system and add that to the product line and differentiate ourselves from other career companies that can't bring that to the table."

Molendorp continued: "Pioneer Mutual brings a brand-new distribution system to the table, personal producing general agents. These people are primarily in the northwest part of the country, where we are not strong geographically. It's a good match. And we can take their principal product, universal life, back across the distribution system, not have to manufacture it, not have to buy a system to administer it, and even strengthen our product line more.

"Our individual line then has ordinary life, fixed universal life, variable

Attendees at AUL's 1965 sales convention on Mackinac Island, Michigan, gathered for this group photo in front of the majestic Grand Hotel.

universal life, fixed annuities, variable annuities, long-term care, impaired-risk products. That competes very nicely against other career companies that don't bring that to the table, let alone adding 401(k), 457, 403(b), tax-deferred annuities, and with what the group folks can add, provide our representatives with a formidable product portfolio."

In 2001 the individual division was renamed individual operations to reflect the expanded scope of the mutual insurance holding company and growing list of partner companies who report through the individual line of business, including OneAmerica Securities, Inc. OneAmerica Securities is a full-service broker dealer for registered representatives, registered investment advisors, and financial planners. It is the first enterprise entity to carry the OneAmerica name. Its predecessor, AUL Equity Sales Corporation, was founded in 1969.

In addition to selling individual products, AUL's career agents also sell some of the 401(k), tax-deferred annuity, and group business.

Moe Silverman said, "Mike Schneider [a retirement services sales representative] is the most knowledgeable guy I know in the 401(k) business, and he is very good in front of the client. So what Moe has to be is a bird dog. I have sat through enough of Mike's interviews when I bring him to my people that I know a fair amount about 401(k). But it is comforting to know that Mike's there and, when we get into some technical issues, he's always got the right answers."

Whether the products are individual, group, or retirement services, AUL continues to rely on knowledgeable people to make the sale, and that isn't likely to change in the future.

In May 2002, the first-ever meeting for the distribution systems of all the

OneAmerica partner companies was held in Indianapolis. More than four hundred representatives of AUL, State Life, and Pioneer Mutual attended the "National Education Conference" (NEC). Respected speakers from throughout the industry spoke from the main platform as did Indianapolis Colts quarterback Peyton Manning. The NEC was very well received, and will become an annual event for OneAmerica partner companies' distribution systems.

"The OneAmerica National Education Conference was an opportunity for us to truly embrace the enterprise concept, inviting our field partners from AUL, PML, State Life, and OneAmerica Securities," said Pete Adkins, vice president of individual marketing. "The result was a top-notch event that has set the stage for future enterprise collaboration."

As Silverman phrased it, "I think AUL will cultivate many systems for delivering its product, but I don't think they are abandoning the agency system. I still think they want to go back to our conventional approach of hiring people, bringing them into the business, training them and building manpower to go out and make direct calls on people. I don't think the bank will be terribly successful relying on people to come through the door and walk up to the insurance window."

Molendorp agrees: "We produce products that compete in the marketplace, and when we add the advice, counsel and work of a representative, they are then the best products the customer can buy. We are not trying to compete strictly on price. We're trying to compete on price plus advice, and that part of our mission hasn't changed."

Galen Meyers, of Overland Park, Kansas, with AUL since 1959, is the only agent ever to have more than $100 million of life insurance in force with the company. For many years, Meyers was a career agent in Topeka, Kansas, where he consistently led the company in applications written. He has been a member of the Million Dollar Round Table since 1961 and has qualified for every AUL business conference for which he was eligible.

CHAPTER 15

A Leader in the Community

The Knights of Pythias lodge was founded on the principles of friendship, charity and benevolence, and employees of American United Life Insurance Company and its predecessor companies have always been active in the community. But, in recent years, the commitment of AUL and its people to Indianapolis and the other communities in which it operates has grown rapidly as well.

Jerry Semler said he believes a real connection with the community began with Clarence Jackson, who started the AUL signboards and who was personally well known and involved in the community. At that same time, J. Howard Alltop was also an influential leader in the community as well as within the company. He had joined American Central in 1931. By 1952 he was secretary of the company. In 1953 he was elected to the board of directors. And in both 1953 and 1954, he served as campaign chairman for the Indianapolis Community Chest, predecessor of the United Way. He was also a leader in alumni affairs at his alma mater, Indiana University.

Later, Jack Reich was also very involved in the community, serving on the boards of many community organizations. *The Indianapolis Star* at one time listed him as one of the most influential leaders in the community. And the company's move into the AUL Tower downtown gave it a greater presence in the community.

Today, Jerry Semler is also extremely active in the community, and in addition, he has had a major influence on the nature and the level of the company's philanthropic activities.

In 1976 AUL established an educational matching gift program for its employees, directors, agents, general agents and retirees. It began to match dollar-for-dollar individual gifts to all accredited colleges and universities, with a minimum of $25 and a maximum of $100 per person a year. In 1992, it extended the program to cover high schools in Marion County, Indiana, and all the counties contiguous to Marion County. The limits have been increased gradually over the years to the point where the company matches all such gifts of $25 or more, to an annual limit of $7,500 per person. In recent years, the company has been matching about $250,000 in gifts each year to about 100 different educational institutions.

In 1980 the company established a Clifford Charitable Trust with $1.4 million. Interest on the money was used to make charitable contributions. That trust automatically dissolved in 1991 after eleven years, with the principal reverting to the company. But in 1985, the company created the AUL Foundation as a permanent philanthropic arm, with the company contributing to it in good years so that it could maintain a level of contributions even in years when its net income level dropped.

In 1982, the year it moved downtown, AUL for the first time made charitable contributions totaling more than 2 percent of its pretax net income. In 1985 it became a member of the Indianapolis Chamber of Commerce's new Two Percent/Five Percent Club, recognizing companies that consistently contribute at least 2 percent of their pre-tax income to charitable, educational, religious, and civic projects.

Since the early years of the United Way annual campaign, AUL and its employees have been major supporters. Each year AUL employees participate in the community-wide campaign in a number of volunteer capacities, and they conduct a major campaign within the company. AUL provides payroll deductions for employee contributions and makes a significant corporate gift. In recent years that gift has been a match of whatever contributions the employees make.

"After we did the matching gifts for colleges," Semler said, "we later moved to match our employee giving to United Way as our corporate gift. I think that was a big milestone. By using the match, we encouraged our employees to reach for higher levels of giving with the idea that the company would match their gift to United Way."

That action by AUL's board actually caused both employee and company giving to the United Way to increase. In 2001 AUL employees pledged close to $300,000. With AUL's match the total United Way contribution was almost $600,000. Most of that money went to the United Way of Central Indiana, but for AUL employees working in other parts of the country, their gifts and the corporate match go to their local United Way.

Because of AUL's community involvement and because of the mergers and acquisitions that have reduced the number of large Indianapolis-based businesses, AUL's leadership role has become more visible, Semler said, and, while AUL wants to continue to maintain giving at a level above the average for corporate America, the company has to be focused and set priorities. Education and the United Way organizations are the top priorities, he said.

For many years, AUL contributed to the Life and Health Insurance Medical Scientist Scholarship Fund, a program of the insurance industry. In 1973, it funded its first of several students at the Indiana University School of Medicine through that fund.

In 1992, with gifts directly to the Indiana University School of Medicine, it began funding a four-year scholarship for students at the Medical School's Bowen Research Center, named in honor of former Indiana Governor Otis R.

Bowen, a family practice physician from Bremen, Indiana. A new four-year scholarship is presented each year to a first-year student.

AUL worked closely with the Bowen Research Center to develop a scholarship that would not only meet the center's goals of fostering preventive medicine, enhancing the availability of rural health care and containing costs, but would also promote the importance of primary care medicine and keep talented medical students in Indiana upon graduation.

In 1991, with a $200,000 gift to the Indianapolis-Marion County Public Library Foundation, AUL endowed a free public lecture series featuring prominent business authors. That gift has brought to Indianapolis such notable authors and speakers as Louis Ruykeyser, Jane Bryant Quinn, George J. W. Goodman ("Adam Smith"), William F. Buckley, Jr., James A. Taylor, and George Will.

After establishing the AUL Foundation in 1985, the company used the foundation to begin contributing $1 million to Indiana University to endow a chair in the IU School of Business in Indianapolis. It was part of the company's

Ronald D. Anderson, Ph.D., (center) is the American United Life Professor of Business Administration at the Indiana University School of Business in Indianapolis. The chair is endowed by a gift from the AUL Foundation. Dr. Anderson was installed in the chair in 1988, when this picture was taken. With him here are graduate students Joe Pfaff and Deborah True.

Teresa Cox (left) and Theresa Peterman ring bells at the Greenwood Mall to help raise money for the Salvation Army holiday fundraiser. The two were among the many AUL employees who have volunteered at a number of locations throughout the Indianapolis area to assist in this worthy cause.

AUL board member James Morris (far left) and Chairman Jerry Semler (second from left) attended the Holy Cross School dedication with the Most Reverend Daniel Buechlein, Archbishop of Indianapolis, and Indianapolis Mayor Bart Peterson. AUL and IWC Resources, of which Morris was chairman and chief executive officer, donated the flagpole and the United States flag for the new inner-city parochial school, which opened in August 2001. The two companies did the same thing the previous year for Holy Angels School, on the city's near Westside.

Jerry D. Semler (center) received the Million Dollar Round Table Foundation's "Circle of Life" award at a dinner in Indianapolis on March 6, 2000. The award was created by the foundation to pay tribute to individuals "whose generosity and compassion extend far beyond themselves to touch many lives," and in Semler's honor the MDRT Foundation donated $100,000 to Riley Hospital for Children. With Semler at the award ceremony are Guy E. Baker, CLU, MSFS (left), 2000 MDRT Foundation president, and Reginald N. Rabjohns, CLU, ChFC, 1999 MDRT president.

The Spirit of America, a 30-by-70-foot walking American flag, has represented American United Life at many public events since its creation by Expo Design in 1996. AUL employees, friends and family members have carried the flag at many events, including the 500 Festival and Veterans Day parades, at the Cherry Blossom Festival in Macon, Georgia, and the 2001 World Police and Fire Games. Thirty-six people are required to carry the flag and at least four more to provide support for the flag team. AUL's flag team coordinator, Shari Morey, said she has no trouble finding volunteers to keep the flag flying—or walking.

effort to get IU to strengthen its programs at IUPUI, where many AUL employees were students. Since that time, Professor Ron Anderson, a marketing specialist, has filled the AUL Professorship.

In 2000 AUL also endowed a professorship at the IU School of Medicine dedicated to preventive health care, including diseases related to obesity, drug addiction and alcohol abuse. Dr. Douglas McKeag, chairman of the Department of Family Medicine, was named the first AUL Professor of Preventive Health Medicine.

AUL's support of IUPUI was praised by Tamara Zahn, president of Indianapolis Downtown, Inc. In a column published in the *Indianapolis Business Journal* in January 2001, she said, in part: "These AUL Foundation contributions to IUPUI are merely the latest in a long history of support for our community. But make no mistake, these kinds of donations stretch beyond their intended philanthropic good. In addition to helping advance higher education, these investments benefit businesses, businesspeople, and business customers by enhancing our community's reputation, improving its quality of life, and attracting and retaining the best employees possible."

AUL is currently paying on a $1.5 million pledge to Purdue University's endowment fund. That gift is to endow a professor of management chair in Purdue's Krannert School of Management.

AUL Treasurer Ron Fritz said contributions from the company and the foundation in 2001 were divided this way: Education, 40 percent; Health and Welfare, 34 percent; Cultural, 12 percent; Civic and Community, 7 percent, and Other, 7 percent.

An element of AUL's emphasis on education is its employee tuition reimbursement program, which it has had since 1978. In 2001, AUL spent almost $375,000 on tuition reimbursement. During the year, 9 employees earned college degrees, Semler said, and 138 others were working on degrees.

In the early 1990s, AUL was one of twelve local companies that invested in the Circle Centre Mall, which opened in downtown Indianapolis in 1995. At the time, Semler said the investment was sound and the company expected a reasonable return on its investment, but he acknowledged it further represented AUL's commitment to downtown Indianapolis.

AUL employees reflect their company's commitment to their community, and many serve on boards and committees of community organizations. Others participate in special activities, such as helping carry AUL's huge walking American flag, which is seen annually in the 500 Festival Parade and other events.

And Semler leads by example. He is a member of many boards of directors of community groups, and he has chaired major fund drives for several of these organizations.

Among the community boards on which he serves or has served are those of the Boy Scouts of America Crossroads Council, Catholic Community Foundation, Center for Leadership Development, Indiana State and Indianapolis

Chambers of Commerce, Indiana Repertory Theatre, Indianapolis Convention and Visitors Association, Indianapolis Museum of Art, Indianapolis Symphony Orchestra, James Whitcomb Riley Memorial Association, Marian College, NCAA Foundation, and the United Way of Central Indiana. He is also a member and past chairman of the Purdue University President's Council.

"One of our ASPIRE values," Semler said, "is excellence: 'We will be distinguished as a quality company and a good corporate citizen.' This will be a very important part of our company's mission and values as we move forward."

In 2001 AUL was the title sponsor of the Indiana Historical Society's Living Legends dinner. This annual fund-raising event honored a number of Indiana's "living legends," including Cartoonist Jim Davis of Muncie, shown here receiving his award from Garfield and James Freeman, AUL's vice president for corporate communications. Former Governor Otis R. Bowen was among others honored during the event.

Syndicated columnist George Will was the sixth distinguished author to give a free public lecture in Indianapolis on a program sponsored by AUL and the Indianapolis-Marion County Public Library. The AUL Business Lecture series was funded by a $200,000 gift to the library from the AUL Foundation in 1991.

Through all kinds of weather since 1984, four sculpted bronze musicians—a pianist, violinist, cellist, and French horn player—have been permanent fixtures in the courtyard of the AUL Tower. Creations of artist Mike Cunningham, they stand on limestone pedestals at the edge of the courtyard reflecting pool. Former AUL Chairman Jack Reich claimed the musicians represented AUL's long-standing support for the Indianapolis Symphony Orchestra, which moved downtown the same year the figures arrived.

Ed Genier, AUL vice president for real estate for many years, was also the unofficial curator of the company's art collection. He knew and loved art and was personally involved in the selection and purchase of many of the 478 pieces the company owns. Even after his retirement in 1995, Genier continued to take a great interest in the collection. Here, he poses with a Brown County landscape by impressionist Adolph Robert Shulz. Genier died unexpectedly on May 18, 2000.

CHAPTER 16

ONEAMERICA FINANCIAL PARTNERS

ONEAMERICA™
Financial Partners

In 2002 AUL and its partner companies introduced a new identity under the OneAmerica "banner."

AUL
a ONEAMERICA™ *financial partner*

All partner companies carry the tagline ***a* ONEAMERICA™ *financial partner*** below the banner and the company name.

Where is American United Life Insurance Company likely to go in the next few years? That's not too difficult to surmise when you see the framework the company has been building for the last few years. In the first decade of the twenty-first century, AUL is going to be busy growing the American United Mutual Insurance Holding Company that it worked so hard to get.

After about three years of effort, the holding company was set in place on December 17, 2000, which was sixty-four years to the day after the completion of the merger, between American Central Life Insurance Company and United Mutual Life Insurance Company, that produced AUL.

As part of the conversion to the new structure, AUL became a stock insurance company wholly owned by a newly incorporated intermediate stock company, OneAmerica Financial Partners, Inc. OneAmerica is wholly owned by American United Mutual Insurance Holding Company. Policyholders who previously held membership voting rights in AUL now have membership voting rights in the holding company, which is still a mutual company. The former AUL board of directors is now the board of the holding company.

Pioneer Mutual Life Insurance Company converted to a stock insurance company under the American United Mutual Insurance Holding Company and OneAmerica on January 1, 2002. CNL Financial Corporation/Cherokee National Life Insurance Company of Macon, Georgia, was a stock company purchased by AUL in December 2000, so it is a subsidiary of AUL. OneAmerica Securities, Inc., formerly AUL Equity Sales Corporation, is also a subsidiary of AUL.

Jerry Semler said he expects State Life, Pioneer Mutual, and CNL/Cherokee National Life all to continue to operate under their own names, selling their own product lines as well as those of the other OneAmerica companies. Each also has a different distribution system, from which all the companies can benefit, he said.

For AUL the driving force is likely to continue to be variable products, with multiple investment options. Semler said each of AUL's product divisions have, or are getting, new administrative operating systems that will allow AUL to compete in this sophisticated market.

"The 401(k) and other retirement plan business," Steve Radcliffe said, "is probably the main franchise of AUL right now, and I think it will continue to be because of the demographics. People are putting away money for retirement. That need is going to accelerate over the next twenty or thirty years. So, just by the sheer demographics, that's going to be an important franchise for us."

Technology is needed to support the sales and servicing of variable products. It is also essential to take full advantage of the Internet. AUL already has much of the infrastructure and is planning to spend millions more on technology in the next few years.

Also, in 2002, when AUL and its mutual insurance holding company subsidiaries and affiliates introduced new logos and a new corporate identity, each company adopted the tagline ***a*** ONEAMERICA™ ***financial partner*** as part of its name and graphic looks. "Partnership, in many forms, is truly one of the main character traits of this organization," said James W. Freeman, vice president of corporate communications.

Asked to comment on the significance of being a 125-year-old company, Radcliffe said, "Certainly, there is an element of pride there, being an organization that has lasted. It justifies and reinforces the core of the values of

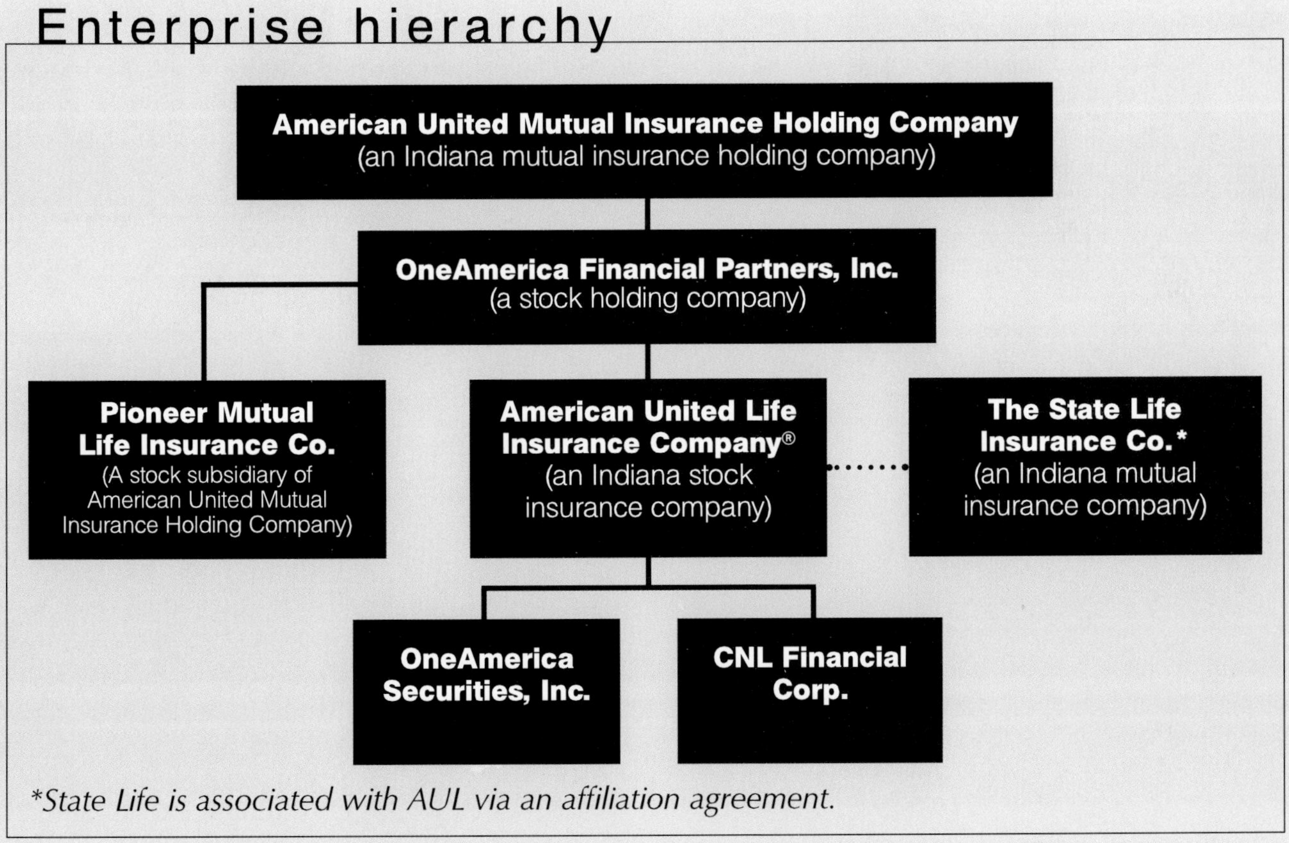

The company has a new structure under the mutual insurance holding company law.

OneAmerica Financial Partners is the name that will tie all of the entities together. Each company will operate under its present name, but each will also identify itself as "*a* OneAmerica *financial partner.*"

Members of the board of directors of American United Mutual Insurance Holding Company: (Seated, from left) Frank D. Walker, James E. Dora, Dr. Steven C. Beering, David W. Goodrich, Arthur L. Bryant, and Yvonne Shaheen. (Standing, from left) Thomas E. Reilly, Jr., John C. Scully, Otto N. Frenzel III, William R. Riggs, Christel DeHaan, James M. Cornelius, William P. Johnson, James T. Morris, R. Stephen Radcliffe, and Jerry D. Semler.

this company to do things for the long run, to manage our affairs and our policyholders' money with a long-term view. I like being a part of that. One of the reasons that we are hesitant to offer stock is that companies that are in the stock market are more focused on short-term results, and that does not match up well with our view of how the insurance business ought to be run. We don't want to manage just for quarterly earnings. We want to manage to be around for another 100 years, and those two are not always in concert."

Semler said, "I think as good stewards of the company, from the board level and senior management level, we want to be able to grow all of our businesses, but we want to be sure we are using our capital efficiently. So, we want to invest and grow business lines that help us get to critical mass and also better returns."

Semler also made a bold prediction: "I'd say we look forward in the next ten years to more than doubling our assets under management to $25 billion. I think that's the reach for us. If at the end of our 125th year, we are at $12 billion, that's doable. That's doubling. The stock market has a lot of effect on our asset base because we are holding separate accounts, but if the market does well over the next ten years. . . ." He didn't complete the sentence, but his meaning was clear.

ACKNOWLEDGMENTS

When I went to work for American United Life Insurance Company in 1974, Jack Reich told me that one of my first responsibilities was to begin planning a hundredth anniversary celebration for the company. The company would be one hundred years old in 1977 and, as part of the observance of that occasion, Mr. Reich wanted a company history.

Fortunately, some of the work on a corporate history had already been done. As far back as 1964, the Twenty-Year Club under Mager Dickson began collecting old photographs for the publication, and in the mid-1960s two free-lance writers, Hortense Myers and Ruth Burnett, interviewed a number of people and put together a first draft of a book.

In 1977 *From the Days of Knights* was published. Georgianne Strange, a member of the AUL public relations department (now corporate communications) pulled it together and wrote the final manuscript. Dr. Alexander Jones, a member of the AUL board of directors at the time, edited that manuscript.

So, when Jerry Semler asked if I would write an up-to-date history for the company's 125th anniversary in 2002, I already had a history with AUL history.

This book draws heavily on the earlier work, including the research done by Hortense Myers and Ruth Burnett. I was particularly pleased to find readable notes from a 1967 interview with Herbert Woollen, who ran American Central and then AUL from 1912 to 1940. He died in 1971 at the age of ninety-five. I also found an article written in 1965 by Eva Woddell McCarthy, who worked for the company from July 1927 to November 1971.

At the suggestion of Cecil Willis, a long-time member of the Knights of Pythias, I tracked down a copy of *A Pythian History* by William D. Kennedy, published in 1904. With it, I was able to supplement the material about the Knights of Pythias insurance program.

For the more recent history, I drew heavily on interviews with AUL employees, AUL agents, former employees, retirees, and others who are part of the company's history. These people included John Barbre, John Barton, Keith Bennett, Judy Boyle, Bob Brady, Eugene Busche, John Cantu, James Comstock, Ron Fritz, Max Hittle, Harold Ingersoll, Scott Kincaid, John Lauter, Chuck Lineback, and Tom Linzer. Also, Galen Meyers, Dayton Molendorp, L. S. Norman, Steve Radcliffe, Jean Reich, Leland Schmitt, David

Schweitzer, Jerry Semler, James Shanahan, Morris "Moe" Silverman, Dolores Smith, Ken Sneed, Don Spence, William Tindall, J. Harold Thompson, Kevin Weston, and K. B. Wilson.

Harold Thompson, who began working for American Central in 1932 and retired from AUL in 1977, and L. S. Norman, whose career at AUL ran from 1949 to 1977, not only granted me lengthy interviews but also read and critiqued drafts of my manuscript.

Two other AUL retirees, Dorothy Claytor and Dolores Smith, loaned me pictures, scrapbooks of clippings, and other personal memorabilia. And former Indianapolis Mayor William H. Hudnut III, who played an important part in getting AUL into a new building downtown, wrote an article that appears in the book.

Many other persons provided valuable assistance by helping me find documents, photographs, dates and other data, and I am grateful to all who assisted. Special thanks to James Adams, who took many of the pictures for the book, and who pulled many others out of his files, and helped me track down still others that were in storage closets and elsewhere; James W. Freeman, who wrote the foreword and served as an adviser and editor; and Jerry Semler, who first suggested the book and then made it all possible. Thanks also to Nancy Baxter of Guild Press Emmis Publishing for not only getting the book published but also providing much advice, counsel, and editing help along the way; Sheila Samson for the design and layout of the interior of the book; and Richard Listenberger, who designed the dust jacket.

In writing this book, I tried not to tell readers more than they want to know and to make the story interesting. But, most important, my goal was to describe how and why the company is where it is today—125 years after the Knights of Pythias lodge introduced a simple life insurance program for its members.

James R. Hetherington
May 2002

American United Mutual Insurance Holding Company

Board of Directors

Jerry D. Semler, CLU, Chairman of the Board, President and Chief Executive Officer

Steven C. Beering, MD, President Emeritus of Purdue University and Chairman of the Purdue Research Foundation, West Lafayette, Indiana

Arthur L. Bryant, FSA, Retired President of The State Life Insurance Company

James M. Cornelius, Chairman of the Board, Guidant Corporation, Indianapolis, Indiana

Christel DeHaan, President and Founder of the Christel DeHaan Family Foundation and Retired Chairwoman and CEO of Resort Condominiums International, Indianapolis, Indiana

James E. Dora, Chairman of the Board and Chief Executive Officer of General Hotels Corporation, Indianapolis

Otto N. Frenzel III, Chairman of the Executive Committee of National City Bank, IN, Indianapolis, Indiana

David W. Goodrich, President and Chief Executive Officer of Central Indiana Corporate Partnership, Indianapolis, Indiana

William P. Johnson, Chairman Emeritus of Goshen Rubber Companies, Inc., Goshen, Indiana

James T. Morris, Executive Director of the United Nations World Food Programme, Rome, Italy

R. Stephen Radcliffe, FSA, CLU, MAAA, Executive Vice President

Thomas E. Reilly, Jr., Chairman of the Board of Reilly Industries, Inc., Indianapolis, Indiana

William R. Riggs, Partner, Ice Miller, Indianapolis, Indiana

John C. "Jack" Scully, CLU, President Emeritus, LIMRA International, Hartford, Connecticut

Yvonne H. Shaheen, Chief Executive Officer and President of Long Electric Company, Indianapolis, Indiana

James M. Swedback, Chairman of Pioneer Mutual Life Insurance Company

Frank D. Walker, Chairman of the Board of Walker Information, Indianapolis, Indiana

Fund Management

Below are the members of AUL's Fund B board of managers and the directors of the OneAmerica Series Fund, Inc., who oversee the management of investments offered to fund AUL's variable products.

R. Stephen Radcliffe (chairman), AUL Executive Vice President

Ronald D. Anderson, Professor of Business Administration, Indiana University

Alpha Blackburn, President and CEO of Blackburn Architects, Inc., Indianapolis, Indiana

James W. Murphy, Retired Senior Vice President, AUL Corporate Finance

Donald J. Stuhldreher, Former President of Capital Markets Group, Vice Chairman of Asset Liability Committee and President of The Huntington Company

Directors of American United Life Insurance Company

1937–2002

J. Howard Alltop	1952–1969
George A. Bangs	1937–1949
F. Leslie Barlet	1977–1979
Earl B. Barnes	1937–1950
Burton E. Beck	1965–1976
Steven C. Beering	1990–
Carroll H. Blanchar	1966–1980
Arthur L. Bryant	1994–
Russell T. Byers	1937–1945
J. DeWitt Carter	1945–1955
Alden P. Chester	1953–1967
Wendell P. Coler	1937–1946
James M. Cornelius	1996–
John W. Craig	1937–1938
Leslie E. Crouch	1937–1964
Christel DeHaan	2000–
James E. Dora	1989–
Frank H. Dunn	1941–1964
David K. Easlick	1971–1990
Donald F. Elliott	1983–1992
Floyd R. Fisher	1947–1952
Otto N. Frenzel	1946–1970
Otto N. Frenzel, III	1971–
David W. Goodrich	1995–
John W. Hillenbrand	1968–1970
Edward A. Horton	1937–1953
Harry T. Ice	1952–1982
Harold G. Ingersoll	1968–1995
Clarence A. Jackson	1946–1967
Frederick G. Jaicks	1972--1978
William A. Jenkins	1939–1951
William P. Johnson	1978–
Alexander E. Jones	1966–1991
Edward M. Karrmann	1947–1968
George A. Kuhn, Jr.	1966–1991
Lawrence Leland	1962–1965
Freda L. Lockhart	1977–1995
Dihl H. Lucus	1968–1971
Alva M. Lumpkin	1937–1940
Frank E. McKinney, Sr.	1970–1972
Frank E. McKinney, Jr.	1977–1992
Richard L. Meares	1939–1952
James T. Morris	1987–
L. S. Norman	1958–1977
William R. O'Neal	1937–1944
Gwynn F. Patterson	1937–1945
Edgar W. Pattison	1980–1987
Earl B. Pulse	1956–1958
R. Stephen Radcliffe	1991–
Samuel N. Regenstrief	1967–1982
Jack E. Reich	1957–1991
Thomas E. Reilly, Jr.	1990–
William R. Riggs	1992–
Leonard D. Schutt	1991–1997
John C. Scully	1997–
Jerry D. Semler	1980–
Yvonne H. Shaheen	1993–
Eber M. Spence	1949–1968
Alfred J. Stokely	1968–1986
Richard B. Stoner	1976–1993
James M. Swedback	2002–
Wallace C. Tomy	1948–1950
Frank J. Travers	1953–1967
Frank D. Walker	1994–
James E. Watson	1937–1947
Harry R. Wilson	1937–1967
Richard S. Witte	1937–1938
Donald E. Wood	1968–1989
Herbert M. Woollen	1937–1967
David G. Wylie	1950–1965
J. Richard Zapapas	1982–1997

INDEX